MARKET STRUCTURE ANALYSIS

James H. Myers
university of southern california

Edward Tauber
carnation company

AMERICAN MARKETING ASSOCIATION

222 S. Riverside Plaza • Chicago, Illinois U.S.A. • (312) 648-0536

Cover design by Mary Jo Galluppi

Library of Congress Cataloging in Publication Data

Myers, James H.
    Market structure analysis.

    1. Marketing—Statistical methods.
    2. Marketing research—Statistical methods.
I. Tauber, Edward M. 1943-   joint author.
II. American Marketing Association.
III. Title.
HF5415.125.M93   658.8′001′82   77-5773
ISBN 0-87757-089-2

TABLE OF CONTENTS

FOREWORD

One of the major developments in marketing in the 1960s was the application of various types of quantitative techniques to the solution of marketing problems and to marketing planning tasks. Of all the different techniques used, the most successful were those involving "multivariate statistical analysis." While it cannot be said that techniques of this type have revolutionized marketing planning or problem solving, they have been of real assistance to *many* companies for *some* types of applications. This usefulness has grown rapidly through the 1960s and the early 1970s.

In spite of this growth, the current contribution of multivariate statistical analysis to market problem solving and planning is, in our opinion, far less than it should be. There appear to be two major reasons for this. First, relatively few researchers are experienced in both the technical *and* managerial aspects of applying the proper techniques to the right problems in ways useful to the market planner. Second, most market planners (marketing vice-presidents and directors, product managers, product planners) simply are not aware of the total spectrum of multivariate techniques and the types of problems to which they are applicable.

The primary objective of this book is to inform market planners of some of the more useful multivariate statistical techniques that have found wide application to marketing during the past fifteen years. The book is organized around applications, not techniques. The latter are incidental to the planner and can be found in a multitude of statistical textbooks and reference materials. The planner needs to know *what* can be done, not *how* it is done. Besides, in many cases several different statistical techniques can accomplish the same objective anyway.

The various applications covered in this book have been developed over the years without a single unifying concept or theme. Different technologies were developed by different scholars at different times to meet a wide variety of planning and problem-solving needs. The only common denominator is that all applications discussed in this book use multivariate statistical methods of one kind or another to *organize in some way a large number of separate aspects of consumer behavior.* Since the goal of this organization is always to produce some sort of coherent framework or "order" out of various aspects of consumer behavior, we will refer to these as efforts to provide "structure" for market planning purposes; hence the title *Market Structure Analysis* for this book.

We feel that market structure analysis has far more promise than has been realized to date. As the practice of marketing inevitably becomes more and more quantitative in the years ahead, the techniques and approaches discussed in this book must become more widely used by professional market planners. These techniques provide answers that cannot be gained in any other way. We hope that this book will help bring about better understanding and greater use of market structure analysis technologies.

We wish to give special thanks to Professors Yoram Wind and Paul Green of the Wharton School, University of Pennsylvania; Professor Volney Stefflre of the University of California, Irvine; and Dr. Edward W. Forgy, statistical consultant, Los Angeles. Professor Wind read the entire manuscript and offered many constructive suggestions about organization, format, and content. Professor Green reviewed Chapter 3 since he, more than any other single person, has been responsible for the introduction of MDS technology into marketing. Professor Stefflre reviewed an early draft of the entire manuscript and especially Chapter 7, "market structure studies" which describes his own process. Dr. Forgy contributed some of the multivariate statistical techniques reported in this book (see especially Chapters 4 and 6) and served as an invaluable technical resource to the senior author of this book. Without his tutelage in statistical technology over the years, this book could not have been wirtten.

James H. Myers
Edward M. Tauber
Los Angeles, Calif., 1976

Chapter 1

STRUCTURING MARKETS

Why Structure Markets?

Businessmen have long seen the need to "structure" markets in which they were competing. In most industries, a great variety of firms serve an even greater variety of customers. It is almost impossible to find a market situation where all buyers choose a particular product or brand for essentially the same reason. Likewise, the diversity of pricing, promotional, and distribution alternatives used by competitors yields a complex maze of firms, people, and products.

Faced with such complexity, humans have the desire to simplify, organize, and structure a framework by which meaning and regularity can be inferred. Structuring markets offers the businessman insights into the interrelationships of firms, people, and products so that he may better *understand* and *predict* consumers' (and possibly competitors') responses to his actions. He is thereby able to make sounder strategic and tactical marketing decisions.

A conceptual model of early structural relationships is shown in Figure 1.[1]

Figure 1.1

EARLY CONCEPTUAL FRAMEWORK

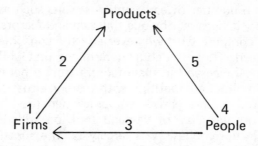

[1]Government was intentionally omitted from this model for simplification, but the increasing involvement of government in business may necessitate its inclusion in a realistic structure.

These relationships reveal how businessmen have attempted to structure markets over time. Table 1.1 shows the various structural efforts in chronological order.

Table 1.1

CHRONOLOGY OF EFFORTS TO STRUCTURE MARKETS

Relationship	Type of Structure	Approx. Dates
How:		
1. Firms relate to other firms	Economists' structure of industry	1930s
2. Firms relate to products	Marketing mix	1950s
3. People perceive firms	Corporate image	1950s
4. People relate to other people	Segmentation	1960s
5. People relate to products	Behavioral market structure	1960s

Early Efforts to Structure Markets

Initially, markets were structured from the supply side. Economists classified markets by the number and types of firms in an industry, using measures of size, concentration, and similarity of competing *firms* (no. 1 in Figure 1.1).

However, in a number of early antitrust suits such as the Dupont cellophane case, it became obvious that demand factors were critical also. Products compete with whatever else the consumer sees as filling a similar need. Thus, the court determined that while cellophane differed in appearance and in manufacture from other wrapping materials, it was in direct competition with them in situations where the customer desired a "protective wrapping" benefit. Thereafter, the concept of cross-elasticity of demand took on added significance. Unfortunately, the emphasis was largely on the substitutability of products as a function of price. Factors such as promotion, differing product benefits, and the like were ignored or lumped into a category called *nonprice* competition.

2

As marketers entered the picture, their needs for structuring markets differed from those of economists. Since they were not primarily concerned with public policy issues but rather with what competitive actions they could take to boost sales or profits, marketers focused on the elements that came to be called the *marketing mix.* This concept produced a new structuring of markets based on *firms'* relationships to *products* (no. 2 in Figure 1.1).

These early attempts to subdivide or structure markets were based on the four basic marketing mix variables: price, product, distribution, and promotion. Thus, successful product or service entries into the market were quickly followed by competitors with products that were similar but differed (sometimes widely) in price, product features or characteristics, distribution channels, and promotion appeals. Management adjusted the marketing mix to give consumers as wide a choice set as possible within profit constraints. Smith referred to this as the market strategy of "product differentiation," the focus still largely on supply factors [3].

This view of markets prevailed in the 1950s and was understandable given the situation then. Millions of families who, for the first time, had considerable discretionary income represented a quickly growing market for durables, convenience items, and the like. New and differentiated product entries met success in an environment of consumer ability to pay for whatever was new and interesting. As markets matured, however, brands proliferated and consumers lost interest in the "new" for its own sake. Being different was not enough. A brief period occurred when firms were largely concerned about their corporate image in the eyes of the public. The proliferation of brands that were all very similar made corporate advertising appealing. Thus, interest centered on how *people* perceived *firms* (no. 3 in Figure 1.1).

Motivation research should be mentioned here, as it was also an important movement during the 1950s. Its objectives were to provide in-depth insights into how people perceived products, what they wanted from products, and why they chose one offering over another. However, motivation research is not included in the elements of market structure discussed in this book, since it made no serious attempt to provide any form of *measurable* (or even conceptual) "structure" for consumer products or services markets. It was essentially a set of unstructured "clinical" diagnostic tools.

Consumer Orientation

The 1960s required a new way of looking at markets. When demand outstrips supply, as it did in the early postwar years, firms generally focus on production issues and the consumer comes last. As the situation shifted from a sellers' to a buyers' market, however, the customer became the focus of the firm's attention. As a result, in the 1960s the marketing concept was *the* philosophy of business. Accompanying this shift was a new approach to structuring markets: market segmentation.

"The concept of segmentation is based on the proposition that *consumers are different* . . . and that these differences are related to differences in market demand." [3] The process is one of disagreating to find differences between potential customers, and then re-aggregating or grouping customers who have one or more of these differences in common. The structure is one of how *people* relate to *each other* (no. 4 in Figure 1.1).

Segmentation is the economists' concept of price discrimination extended to include differences in customers other than their differential reactions to price. Logically, it was the economist who provided a ready storehouse of demographics to start the process of segmenting markets based on characteristics of buyers. Demographic information was readily available from a wide variety of both secondary and primary data sources. Further, all major types of media came to provide this information so that promotion expenditures could reach target markets more accurately and effectively.

It should be noted here that the term *market segmentation* was originally used to refer to *groups of consumers,* homogeneous in some respect (s), who would *respond differently* to a particular marketing mix than other segments or other people in general. Usage of this term over the years, however, has diluted and obfuscated its meaning, so that *market segment* is often erroneously used today to refer to: (1) groups of consumers that are homogeneous in ways that do *not* relate to market response, and (2) groups of marketing *variables or factors* that affect consumer response in some meaningful ways [see 1]. Many of these attempts should more properly be called *market structure* efforts, since their primary objective is not to find groups of consumers but rather to find influencing factors, patterns or relationships among these factors or among items purchased, or other forms of regularities that help to structure a market. (In

4

Chapter 6, an example using findings from a specific product class will show why *market segmentation is only one form of market structure.*)

Behavioral Science Concepts

The 1960s saw major advances in efforts to structure markets in more subtle ways useful for market planning purposes. A wide variety of scholars provided tools and data for such diverse approaches as values and attitudes, life cycle and social class, personality, diffusion theory, risk, opinion leadership, and purchase habits (heavy half, brand loyalty, etc.).

These and other approaches had the common objective of measuring attitudinal, behavioral, and perceptual characteristics of buyers. While these aspects were not as objectively measurable as demographics, they often provided far more insight into buyer behavior and thus into the "structure" of consumer markets.

Benefit Orientation

A fundamental problem with most of these behavioral variables was that they described *how people were different* rather than *why preferences were different.* In the late 1960s structural emphasis shifted from people descriptors to variables that reflected the *relationships of people to products* (no. 5 in Figure 1.1). Segmentation by customer desire for attributes or benefits was one of the first of this type. "The belief underlying this segmentation strategy is that the benefits which people are seeking in consuming a given product are the basic reasons for the existence of true market segments." [2, p. 3]

CURRENT CONCEPTUAL FRAMEWORKS

Out of this process grew the increasingly dominant notion that *consumer needs and objectives constitute the heart of a marketing strategy* and that other factors are important only insofar as they either affect or satisfy these needs. A diagram depicting the various relationships in the current conceptual framework is shown in Figure 1.2. It expands on the fifth stage in Figure 1.1—how people relate to products.

The diagram in Figure 1.2 places at the center such factors as consumer: (1) wants, needs, and objectives; (2) usage patterns; and (3) perceptions and evaluations of competing alternative products. These are represented by the single notation "consumer benefits wanted." The interrelationships of these three aspects of consumer benefits wanted constituted another step in the evolution of market structure analysis (no. 6 in Figure 1.2).

Figure 1.2

CURRENT CONCEPTUAL FRAMEWORK

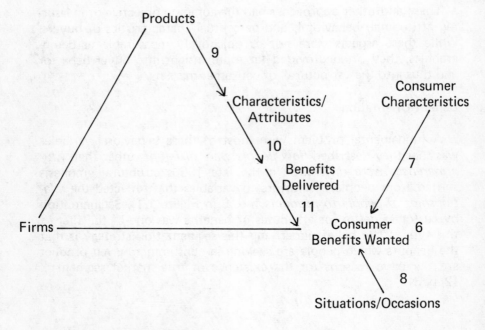

Wants, Needs, and Objectives

In his classic article on benefit segmentation, Haley noted that each segment is identified by the benefits it is seeking. However, it is the total configuration of the benefits sought which differentiates one segment from another, rather than the fact that one segment is seeking one particular benefit and another a quite different benefit. Individual benefits are likely to have appeal for several segments. In fact, the research that has been done thus far suggests that most people would like as many benefits as possible. However, the relative importance they attach to individual benefits can differ importantly and, accordingly, can be used as an effective lever in segmenting markets. [2, p. 32]

Many early benefit segmentation studies measured benefits by directly questioning respondents about what needs were satisfied by particular products or categories. Cluster analysis techniques were used to construct segments in many cases. Other approaches *inferred* what benefits consumers were searching for by examining their usage patterns and/or product perceptions. One such approach is described next.

Usage Patterns

It was probably Stefflre who first attempted to provide a *systematic framework* for organizing and grouping the various types of benefits people want from a particular product class [see 4]. For each study, he constructs from preliminary interviews an "item-use" matrix, consisting of specific products (items) people might use for each of many specific needs (uses) they might have. Then another sample of consumers is asked to complete this matrix—each respondent indicating which products he or she feels are suitable for each use or need. Thus, the respondent might be asked which drugs he or she might use for a variety of physical maladies: a cold, a sore throat, a backache, and so on. These maladies are, in effect, the needs, objectives, or *benefits* people want.

Using a clustering algorithm, Stefflre is able to search for usage patterns for the various products. Thus, groups of uses that are similar in terms of the medicines taken are assumed to be similar in terms of benefits desired. Configurations among these benefit clusters provide a very useful form of structure for a given market, based on product usage.

Perception and Evaluation of Competing Alternative Products

Knowing how consumers perceive competitive offerings in *relation to each other* (in quantitive terms) can also be valuable information for management. Such data provides a *perceptual structure* of the market from the consumer's perspective (a structure of how products relate to other products). A body of technology known as position-

7

ing mapping is built on the premise that psychophysical and statistical techniques of various kinds can be used to:

1. Determine product attributes that are most relevant to consumers in *perceiving* and/or *evaluating* competing brands, products, or service offerings
2. Spatially "position" the competitive items in terms of these relevant attributes, using two- or three-dimensional configurations (each dimension representing an important attribute or feature)
3. Determine characteristics of an ideal product(s) on the basis of consumer preferences for the various attributes and for competing products

The resulting spatial configurations purport to represent the conceptual frameworks consumers bring into play in perceiving and evaluating competing alternatives in the marketplace. An implicit assumption is that the dimensions (axes) of the positioning map represent product attributes controlling, or at least very instrumental in determining choice behavior.

Consumer Behavioral Characteristics

Other parts of Figure 1.2 reflect the different consumer characteristics that affect and determine benefits wanted, as well as the specifics as to how products satisfy these desires. Consumers have been studied in terms of their own behavioral characteristics—psychographics and demographics—and the extent to which these affect needs and objectives, usage patterns, and perceptions and evaluations of products/services (no. 7 in Figure 1.2). Psychographics (life styles) in particular have been studied intensively and include the measurement of people's attitudes, interests, opinions, personality, and values [see 5].

Situations and Occasions

Various research studies have confirmed that the benefits people seek from a product depend on the usage occasion or situation in which they find themselves when they purchase or use it. Thus, "situational segmentation" came into being (no. 8 in Figure 1.2). Often people are basically very similar but have differing product/service needs when in differing *situations*. A situation may be some combin-

8

ation of circumstances—lunch when home with the flu—or it may be a single circumstance, such as dinner on an ordinary evening.

For example, 30 percent of the population may share the situation of being rushed for breakfast, of feeling nutrition at that time is important, and of not being on a diet; however, if only 40 percent of this group eats breakfast, there may be a potential for building a product for the remaining 60 percent. Similarly, if people want essentially the same benefits from a beverage in mid-morning as in mid-afternoon, and if these benefits are quite different from those desired at meals or before bedtime, "between meals" provides a focal point for structuring markets. This market definition may or may not be independent of particular characteristics of consumers.

Product/Service Attributes and Characteristics

Just as consumers came to be analyzed in terms of their distinguishing characteristics, so did products come to be analyzed in terms of the features or attributes of which they were constituted. Early economic jargon had regarded products as "bundles of utilities." The 1960s saw intensive efforts to determine just what these utilities were, which were most important, and how they could best be combined for a particular product/service.

In the late 1960s and early 1970s, computers produced hundreds of correlational studies to establish the relationships of attributes to each other and to various forms of evaluative criteria (such as overall evaluations of products/services, choice among competing brands, and frequency of use). All of this provided additional structure to markets in terms of *product characteristics affecting consumer perceptions and preferences* (no. 9 in Figure 1.2).

In particular, researchers were concerned with the relative importance of the various features of which a particular product/service was composed. Some said the evidence showed clearly that all features were essentially equivalent in importance; therefore, the more desirable features a product had, and the more *of* these desirable features it had, the better. Others pointed out conceptual and methodological problems with the available evidence and maintained that the jury was still out [see 6].

All of this work resulted in more attention being focused on both the types and the importance of the various *benefits* provided by products and services. Thus, product characteristics or attributes were seen as important insofar as they delivered certain benefits to consumers (no. 10 in Figure 1.2). But were the benefits delivered the ones that were *desired* by consumers? This question set the stage for the next form of market structure: benefit structure analysis.

Benefit Structure Analysis

Some recent proprietary studies have suggested that often more can be learned by focusing on *problems* and *deficiencies* of existing products than on the relative importance of constituent features or attributes. This highlights the importance of the gaps between specific benefits people *want* and what they are now able to *obtain* from existing products or services (no. 11 in Figure 1.2).

Until recently there was no systematic plan of inquiry designed to simultaneously identify and measure both the benefits desired and the benefit deficiencies in broad need areas, as opposed to more limited product or service categories. For example, what kinds of new banking services do people need? What kinds of multipurpose home repair tools can they use? What entirely new types of food or beverage products will satisfy presently unmet needs? Note that such needs are defined in terms of very *broad* product or service areas, yet business firms want relatively *specific* answers to use in new product/service development efforts. A technique for developing information of this type is called benefit structure analysis (discussed in Chapter 8).

Benefit structure analysis is designed to accomplish two primary objectives: (1) to identify the *most important consumer needs* within a broad need area and to measure the relative importance of these needs in quantitative terms; and (2) to measure the extent to which each of these important needs is *not now being met,* also in quantitative terms. The needs and deficiencies are considered simultaneously to identify specific opportunities for improving present products or for developing entirely new types of products/services (such as bank credit cards, instant breakfast, etc.).

SCOPE OF COVERAGE

The objective of this book is to explain some of the above approaches to structuring markets that are based on various aspects of consumer behavior as opposed to marketing mix and demographic variables. *Market structure analysis* can be defined as *the search for quantitative frameworks that show the arrangements and interrelationships of the various parts of a market in terms of consumer attitudes, needs, perceptions, product usage, behavioral patterns, and other aspects of consumer behavior.* The purpose is to provide insights for market planning that go beyond the conventional marketing research tools used for many decades prior to the 1960s.

Specifically, this book discusses the following types of market structure:

—Product positioning, based on

    Perceptions

    Preferences

—Market segmentation and other forms of market structure based on

    Perceptions

    Preferences

    Usage and shopping patterns

    Product benefits and attributes wanted

    Perceived problems and deficiencies in present products

    Situational factors surrounding product usage

    Other aspects of consumer behavior

—Market structure studies

—Benefit structure analysis

—Conjoint measurement (Multiple trade-off analysis)

There are many points on which these various approaches are similar or interrelated. For example, product positioning can be done for *all* consumers of a given product type combined, but it is often better first to segment the market in some meaningful way and then to position products for each segment separately. The same is true for conjoint measurement vis-a-vis segmentation. And, both market structure studies and benefit structure analysis use positioning and segmentation technologies as part of their own complete study processes.

Even though these overlaps do exist, each of the approaches listed above constitutes a separate body of technology with its own primary objectives, processes, and tools. All are current by being used by marketing researchers and planners.[2]

Diverse as they seem, these approaches have several things in common:

1. They are based on the basic human processes of perception, motivation, attitudes, and behavior, rather than on demographics or marketing mix variables.

2. They involve the simultaneous consideration of many behavioral variables or sets of variables, requiring "multivariate" (many variables simultaneously) statistical analytic techniques.

3. They provide conceptual frameworks that represent various aspects of the *structure* of a particular market, in *quantitative terms.*

Multiple-Factor vs. Single-Factor Structure

It should be noted that many behavioral factors will not be discussed in this book. Behavioral science constructs such as social class, life cycle, opinion leadership, risk, and others might be termed "single-factor" behavioral considerations since they represent the attempt to adapt a single construct borrowed from psychology, sociology, political science, communications, or any other discipline to the marketing or products. Some constructs were, of course, developed by marketing scholars based on actual or hypothesized market behavioral patterns (e.g., heavy user, brand loyalty, risk). While these constructs would not be relevant for every given product or market, no one can seriously question their contribution to enlarging the scope and understanding of marketing.

However, consideration of these single-factor constructs will be omitted from this book for two reasons: (1) they have already been defined and studied individually in a wide variety of published reports; and (2) they do not necessarily interrelate to form broad conceptual frameworks. Thus, instead of helping to *structure a market,*

---

[2]Except the Stefflre market structure studies.

these constructs might be considered factors that *affect consumer choice decisions.* Many are also likely to be underlying determinants of the types of multiple-factor behavioral market structures that are the primary concern here.

This book will include market segmentation as one form of market structure, but only that segmentation that looks for groups of consumers who are similar in terms of the behavioral factors discussed within the book. We are not concerned here with segments based on demographic, psychographic, life cycle, social class, or other single-factor behavioral variables.

SUMMARY

This book, then, documents the emergence of a new technology: *the application of multivariate analytic techniques to measurements of consumer perception, motivation, and behavior for the purpose of providing useful ways of structuring markets for more effective marketing planning.* Some of the techniques in this book are well known and have been used for many years; others are familiar to relatively few individuals and firms. One of the objectives of this book is to promote greater understanding and usage of all techniques by scholars and business firms dealing with consumer markets.

It should be noted that this new technology is not a substitute for "bread and butter" market research. Market planners should continue to analyze their markets using well-known conventional research tools and techniques. Survey research, observation, and experimentation normally provided the foundation for understanding such basic questions as who uses what products/services for what purposes, at what times, in what quantities; reactions to company promotion efforts; and the like. Planners should start the market-structuring process by learning about demographics, awareness, attitudes, and single-factor behavioral concepts such as family life cycle, family decision making, social class, and risk.

The techniques discussed in this book are more advanced in several senses: they are more appropriate after a firm has a good idea of the basic characteristics of its market; they are complex and consider many marketing variables simultaneously; they require highly trained quantitative research analysts; and they require experienced market planners to translate conceptually difficult research output into practical plans.

It is the hope of the authors that this book will create a greater awareness of the potential utility of techniques for structuring markets as discussed in the following pages. These techniques portend a new era in market planning, one with the ability to understand far more about the basic motivational and behavioral patterns of consumers than conventional marketing research allows. The market planner who does not know and use this new technology is limiting the ability of his firm to cope with the competitive pressures in consumer marketing today.

REFERENCES TO CHAPTER 1

1. Blattberg, Robert C. and Subrata K. Sen. "Market Segmentation Using Models of Multidimensional Purchasing Behavior," *Journal of Marketing.* 38 (October 1974), 17-28.

2. Haley, Russell I. "Benefit Segmentation: A Decision-Oriented Research Tool." *Journal of Marketing,* 32 (July 1968), 30-5.

3. Smith, Wendell. "Product Differentiation and Market Segmentation as Alternating Marketing Strategies," *Journal of Marketing,* 21 (July 1956), 3-8.

4. Stefflre, Volney J. "Some Applications for Multidimensional Scaling to Social Science Problems," in Frank M. Bass, Charles W. King, and Edgar A. Pressemier, eds., *Multidimensional Scaling: Theory and Applications in the Behavioral Sciences,* Vol. 2. New York: Seminar Press, 1972, 211-43.

5. Wells, William D., ed.. *Life Style and Psychographics.* Chicago: American Marketing Assn., 1974.

6. Wilkie, William L. and Edgar A. Pessemier. "Issues in Marketing's Use of Multi-Attribute Attitude Models," *Journal of Marketing Research,* 10 (November 1973), 428-41.

Chapter 2

INTRODUCTION TO SCALING METHODS
FOR PRODUCT POSITIONING

One of the more promising analytical developments during the 1960s was a body of diverse technology known as *multidimensional scaling*. Its purpose was to measure quantitatively the relationships among objects (brands/products/services/firms) in terms of consumers' *perceptions* and *preferences* for these objects. Moreover, it allowed the presentation of relationships in spatial configurations of two or three dimensions, leading to use of the terms *product positioning* and *perceptual mapping*. Green and Carmone note:

> The analysis of buyer perceptions and preferences regarding products and services is congenial with both the marketing concept and market segmentation. First, buyer perception and preference scaling can provide operational measures of how the product or service is being seen and evaluated by the firm's clientele, actual or potential. Second, the fact that neither perceptions nor preferences need be homogeneous over buyers can suggest opportunities for segmentation strategy . . . . Perceptions and preferences are two fundamental phenomena of all human behavior. [2, p. 3]

When perception or preference ratings are analyzed using various multidimensional scaling techniques, the result is a representation in spatial form of the perceived relationships among objects. Thus, spatial distances between any two objects (products/brands/services/firms) represent the degree to which these objects are perceived as being *similar* in terms of relevant features or attributes or in terms of preferences. This form of market structure is commonly referred to as a *positioning map*.

16

Positioning maps consist of three elements:

1. A set of axes or dimensions that represent product features that are "important" in some ways to the consumer

2. A "score" for each product on each of the important features represented by the axes

3. Plots of these scores in two or three dimensions, to produce spatial maps that show at a glance: (a) how similar each product is to every other product, and (b) how much of each of the important features each product is felt to possess

A positioning map for snack foods is shown in Figure 2.1 as an illustration. This map indicates that nutrition and convenience are important in some way to mothers in evaluating snacks to feed to their children; these two features are the axes of the position map. The map also shows how much nutrition and how much convenience each of ten snack foods is believed by mothers to have. The questions *why* and *in what sense* nutrition and convenience are important to mothers, as well as what should be done from a market planning standpoint, are matters that will be discussed in later chapters. At this point it is only necessary to understand what a positioning map looks like and represents, in general terms.

Figure 2

SAMPLE POSITIONING MAP FOR SNACK FOODS

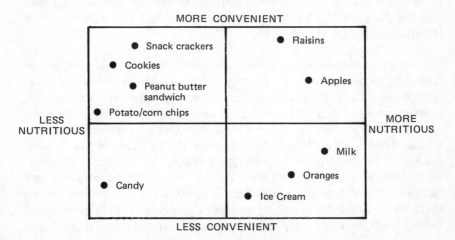

Positioning maps are highly useful in two major ways:

1. *Data reduction:* The almost infinite complexities of similarities and differences within a set of competing products or services can be reduced by identifying the two or three principal features or product characteristics that predominate when consumers either *perceive* or *evaluate* differences among the products.

2. *Display:* Perceptions or evaluations of competing products that are presented in spatial form (two- or three-dimensional figure or map) provide a display that is easily grasped by marketing planners and managers; this makes communication and discussion much easier and more efficient by focusing on those aspects of the product that are most relevant to product and promotion decisions.

Types of Positioning Maps

It is important at this point to note the distinctions between the three generic forms of positioning maps:

- Perceptual
- Preference
- Semantic

Several statistical techniques can be used to construct these various types of maps, and the researcher must select the one or ones that suit his own needs. Many of these technologies are discussed in the following chapters.

Perceptual maps are based on how consumers perceive *similarities and differences* among competing products. These similarities and differences can be measured either in terms of ratings of a set of features or product characteristics common to all products, or by comparing each product as a whole against every other product as a whole. These latter (direct) comparisons can be made either in *rank orders* of similarities or by *ratings of subjective distances* between each pair of products. The axes of the resulting positioning maps represent those features or product characteristics that people notice most in distinguishing among competing products on a perceptual basis. They *may or may not* represent features that these same people want most in a product or that they use as a basis for selecting among products. Perceptual maps portray the "perceptual space" of either a single consumer or of all consumers in a sample.

On the other hand, preference maps show products positioned in relation to those product features or characteristics that people *consider most important* in making overall evaluations of the product or in choosing among competing products. The axes of the map represent the two or three features that are most relevant from the standpoint of consumer preference, and these maps portray the consumer's "preference space."

Since perceptual space and preference space are often not the same, it becomes very important for the marketing manager to *select the type of map that best suits his own particular planning needs.* For the usual competitive situation, with brands competing with one another in a clearly defined product category, the present authors recommend preference maps, since the axes represent product features or characteristics that *make a difference* to the consumer in choice situations and therefore are actionable in terms of product changes or the selection of promotion themes. On the other hand, sometimes the planner wants to understand how people perceive similarities and differences among diverse competing entries in a somewhat ambiguous product area, such as snack foods, alcoholic beverages, suitable sauces for Mexican foods, natural versus synthetic breakfast foods, and the like. In this case a perceptual map would often be preferable as a first step in laying out the entire product area as it is perceived by consumers.

The third type of map, semantic, is produced by a technique (factor analysis) that merely groups together those product attributes that are rated similarly by respondents in describing a set of competing products or services. For example, one of the present authors asked subjects to rate six orange juice-type drinks on fifteen product attributes. Factor analysis of these ratings showed that one of the most clearly defined groupings of similar attributes consisted of: thickness, body, pulp, heaviness. This tells us that these terms all mean about the same thing to people, but *it does not tell us anything at all about how important thickness or body is in evaluating these drinks or in choosing among competing products or brands.* (In fact, correlation analysis showed that none of these features was of any real importance at all to consumers in this study.)

This illustrates the fundamental problem with using factor analysis to construct positioning maps: The entire process is essentially an exercise in semantics. Worse, the investigator can inadvertently predetermine the outcome by his or her selection of the number and degree of similarity of the attributes used to rate products. The more important the researcher feels a particular product feature is (e.g., styling, durability), the more likely he or she is to ask respondents to rate several *aspects* of this feature; hence, the more likely it is that this feature will emerge as a "factor." Since researchers normally use the first factor as the first axis, the second as the second axis, and soon, it is apparent that a semantic map may be useless or misleading for most market planning purposes.

Types of Scaling Technologies Used for Positioning

While there is little disagreement among researchers as to the form and utility of the *output* from perceptual or preference mapping, there is wide diversity regarding the types of *input data* and *statistical technology* used to construct these maps. Usually each researcher tends to settle on a single approach and to use data inputs and statistical tools suitable for this approach. Yet each approach rests on a different set of assumptions, and this can produce major differences in the meaning of resulting positioning maps.

The various positioning technologies in current use can be classified into one of four general types of scaling approaches (listed neither in order of effectiveness nor frequency of use):

- Multidimensional scaling
- Discriminant analytic scaling
- Factor analytic scaling
- Weighted covariance scaling

Subsequent chapters in this book will discuss, compare, and contrast each of these approaches in relation to the others. Each differs in one or more major ways from the others. Even within each approach there is often wide variation in terms of alternative analytic techniques and specific forms of data input (particularly for nonmetric multidimensional scaling). Space does not allow more than a brief introduction to each technology, with special emphasis on comparisons in terms of inputs and analytic procedures, and on the basic assumptions for each approach. (More formal schemes for classifying various types of scaling techniques have been proposed by Coombs [1, pp. 21-28] and by Shepard [3, pp. 23-44].

Basic Principles of Measurement

Fundamental to any discussion of multidimensional scaling is an understanding of measurement *theory* and the four major types of measuring *scales*. Following is a brief review for readers not already familiar with these concepts. Such a review is essential to understanding how the various positioning techniques differ with regard to data input and output.

In a broad sense, measurement consists of assigning numbers to represent different states or levels of some empirical phenomenon. In everyday usage, differences in meaning among various types of numbers are so obvious that there is no need for a "theory of measurement" to explain them. No one would even consider the idea that football player no. 15 was necessarily better than player no. 14 or no. 13; yet no one would argue that $15 normally represents something better and more useful than $14 and less. Thus, numbers can have different meanings in different situations; technically, this translates into the idea that numbers can represent different *types of scales*. The four major types of scales in common usage are, in increasing order of precision:

- *Nominal:* Numbers are used for *identification* only, as in the case of athletic jerseys. Nothing is implied by the relative sizes of numbers—letters or other symbols could serve just as well.

- *Ordinal:* Numbers imply only an ordering of objects according to some criterion, usually a rank ordering. Thus, a rank of 4 is assumed to be superior to a rank of 5 (if 1 is highest) on the basis of some meaningful standard. In the case of positioning studies, ranks are often used to denote degrees of similarity or preference among objects being "scaled."

- *Interval:* Numbers take on added meaning. Whereas with an ordinal scale we do not know if a rank of 7 is *as much* better than a rank of 8 as a rank of 8 is better than a rank of 9, interval scales indicate that this is so; in other words, the interval between 7 and 8 is the same as the interval between 8 and 9. This should be true both for precise physical measuring instruments

21

as well as for "approximate" psychological (or psychophysical) measuring instruments (such as an IQ test).

- *Ratio:* Intervals between numbers are equal *and* there is an absolute zero point denoting a state of total absence of the thing being measured. For example, money is measured on a ratio scale, as are numbers of units produced or consumed. In contrast, mental abilities, interests, and temperament are ordinarily measured on scales that have interval properties (at best). Total absence of any of these is unmeasurable under normal conditions, so there is no zero point. A special form of ratio scale used in the nonmetric scaling discussed in Chapter 3 is the extended ratio scale, which allows both plus *and* minus values from a zero point that is uniquely determined.

All four types of scales are used in the total spectrum of general marketing research, and all are also used in various phases of the market structure research as described in this book. Indeed, one of the major aspects in which various techniques or approaches differ is the type of scale used for either input or output data.

The term *metric* is used here to refer to numbers that have interval or ratio scales; *nonmetric* normally refers to numbers that have at least ordinal properties, although it is also used for scaling methods based on nominal data. These terms will be used frequently throughout the following chapters.

Common Objectives of Multidimensional Scaling Methods

Despite their dissimilarities in terms of input and technology, all scaling approaches in general use have two common objectives. The first is to discover the criteria (product/service attributes) used by respondents in either *perceiving* or *evaluating* a set of objects. These criteria become the axes of the positioning map. The second objective is to locate or "position" each object on each of the axes, usually in either two or three dimensions simultaneously.

The first objective involves determining how many axes or attributes are of primary importance in perceptions or evaluations of objects. Studies covering a wide variety of subject matter (consumer and industrial products, business and professional publications, university curricula, business firms) typically find that two or three dimensions are sufficient to portray relationships among objects with reasonable accuracy. This suggests that, in the aggregate, consumers' evaluations or perceptions are based primarily on a very few *major* attributes or features of a product or service. Other features have only a relatively minor influence on consumers as a whole, although they could have a major influence for one or more subgroups (market segments).

For example, a study by one of the authors showed that in choosing among competing airlines *most* businessmen base their decision on friendliness of personnel plus quality of food. However, these factors may be of lesser importance to some businessmen who are much more interested in on-time record or luggage handling. A positioning map representing all businessmen could be quite different from one representing only a segment who were interested in certain specific services.

The reader who has seen a number of different positioning maps knows that these maps always show their axes or dimensions perpendicular to one another (i.e., orthogonal). The right angles imply that the two or three major criteria (attributes) are *unrelated,* that is, independent of one another. Are they? Sometimes, and sometimes not. Some of the techniques that produce maps provide only for orthogonal axes; others allow axes to be other than at right angles (i.e., oblique). The principal reason maps are shown as orthogonal is because investigators are primarily interested in features or attributes that are as *different* as possible even in cases where this presents a somewhat distorted view of reality.[1]

From a product development standpoint, there is probably merit in using orthogonal axes for nearly all maps. A company is interested in the key *separate* aspects of product or service design. Still, management must keep an open mind on the matter of related features (e.g., a beverage that both "satisfies thirst" and "refreshes") that are very important but are not totally independent of one another. Perceptual maps can easily be drawn with nonperpendicular axes in either two or three dimensions, should this be indicated from the data. This problem can also be handled by using some special types of "property fitting" algorithms.

-----

[1] Another reason is a technical one: Orthogonal dimensions allow the use of a simple Euclidean distance measure—d^2—rather than a more complicated measure such as the Mahalanobis D^2.

23

MDS Technology

While some scaling techniques can be used with either metric (interval or ratio) or nonmetric (ordinal) input data, current usage of the term *multidimensional scaling* (MDS) implies either *nonmetric inputs* or use of the ordinal properties of metric inputs (i.e., converting interval values obtained from respondents into ordinal—rank—values prior to input). This is a major distinction from other perceptual mapping approaches. Chapter 3 will be restricted to discussing data of this type. It is important to note, however, that many MDS techniques can also be used on interval-scaled input data.

REFERENCES TO CHAPTER 2

1. Coombs, C. H. *A Theory of Data,* New York: John Wiley & Sons, 1964.

2. Green, Paul E. and Frank J. Carmone. *Multidimensional Scaling and Related Techniques in Marketing Analysis.* Boston: Allyn & Bacon, 1970.

3. Shepard, Roger N., A. Kimball Romney, and Sara B. Nerlove. *Multidimensional Scaling: Theory and Application in the Behavioral Sciences.* New York: Seminar Press, 1972.

Chapter 3

POSITIONING USING
MULTIDIMENSIONAL SCALING TECHNIQUES (MDS)

While several of the technologies in this book are in fact "multi-dimensional scaling techniques," use of this terminology was pre-empted early in the 1960s by marketing scholars who employed it primarily to refer to *nonmetric* multidimensional scaling (MDS). "The objective of nonmetric multidimensional scaling can be stated somewhat nonrigorously as follows: given a rank order of proximity data, find a spatial configuration whose rank order of (ratio-scaled) distances—in a specified dimensionality—best reproduces the original rank order of the input data." [2, p. 36] Dealing primarily with *perceptual* maps, here we find several items of interest in this definition:

1. Scaling is performed on "proximity" data; that is, the respondent is asked only *how similar* each object (product/brand/firm) is to every other object. This means that all possible *pairs of objects* are rank ordered in terms of their similarity to each other. If there are *n* objects to be scaled there are $n(n-1)/2$ pairs, and all pairs are initially ranked in terms of similarity, from most similar to least similar. The resulting pairing produces the basic *similarities matrix* from which the perceptual map is construct-ed. An example is shown in Table 3.1. (Alternatively, "psycho-logical distances" of each object from every other object can be obtained from respondents on a *metric* scale.)

2. Input data (rankings or ratings from respondents) are given in terms of ranks or are converted into ranks, constituting an ordinal scale.

3. Output is provided in terms of ranks of ratio-scaled distances, indicating an "upgrading" of the data from ordinal to interval scaled or stronger.

4. It is left to the respondent to decide what criteria he or she will use to judge degrees of similarity among objects. No discussion or instructions of any kind precede respondent ratings.

5. The criterion for evaluating how accurately the computer algorithm (computation procedure) has "reproduced" the original rank order of the input is the degree to which the *ranks* of (ratio-scaled) distances between objects on the perceptual map conform to the *ranks* of similarities among pairs of objects based on the original respondent rankings. The computer provides a numerical index indicating goodness of fit.

Nonmetric perceptual maps can be developed from: (1) average ranks from all respondents, (2) average ranks from some segment of respondents homogeneous in some way (e.g., demographics, or similarities matrices, or (3) any single individual respondent. The example that follows was based on all respondents in a sample of physicians. It helps to illustrate the process of nonmetric scaling—from form of original input data, through statistical processing, to final output.

Perceptual Map of Ethical Drugs

The researcher conducting this study [4] was interested in determining the features doctors use in evaluating competing brands of ethical drugs. He believed that perceptions, rather than either preferences or the objective analysis of laboratory reports, could best explain physician selection from among the competing brands. A sample of doctors was asked to compare five brands of drugs commonly prescribed for a particular illness, using the questions shown in Table 3.1. Note that these questions forced the doctors to make *direct comparisons of products against each other* in terms of how similar they are to one another overall. No instructions were given as to what product attributes or features these comparisons should be based on.

The composite of answers from the questions in Table 3.1 was used to construct the single similarities matrix in Table 3.2. This matrix should be interpreted as follows: The "1" entry in the matrix

Table 3.1

ILLUSTRATION OF THE METHODS OF DATA COLLECTION USED IN THE PHYSICIAN STUDY

Method of Triadic Combinations

Instructions: Select the *two* most similar and the two *least* similar brands in each triple.

	Most Similar	Least Similar
Brand A	( )	( )
Brand B	( )	( )
Brand C	( )	( )

All possible combinations of triples [(6!/3!3!) = 20] were included.

Rating Scale Method

Instructions: Compare the five remaining brands to the brand acting as an anchor point by assigning a number which reflects your assessment of their overall similarity to the anchor point brand.

Reference Scale

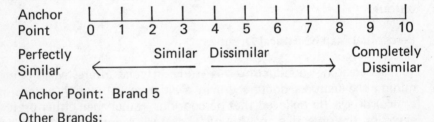

Anchor Point: Brand 5

Other Brands:

Brand 3	Brand 4	Ideal	Brand 2	Brand 1

Scale Value:

| ___ | ___ | ___ | ___ | ___ |

Each brand in turn acted as an anchor point. While interval measures might be derived from this procedure, only the ordinal results were utilized.

Source: J. A. Neidell [4].

indicates that most respondents perceived Drugs 3 and 5 to be the *most similar* of any of the possible pairs of drugs (plus the "ideal" drug); the "2" entry shows that Drugs 2 and 4 were perceived to be *next* most similar on an overall basis; the "15" entry shows that Drug 2 and the "ideal" drug were perceived to be the *least* similar of any pair of drugs in the study.

Table 3.2

SIMILARITIES MATRIX FOR ETHICAL DRUG PRODUCTS

Drug No.	1	2	3	4	5
1					
2	3				
3	8	12			
4	7	2	9		
5	5	11	1	10	
Ideal	14	15	4	13	6

A nonmetric multidimensional scaling analysis of this similarities matrix (using the TORSCA algorithm [see 3]) produced the two-dimensional orthogonal map shown in Figure 3.1. The computer produces the coordinates for the map but does not tell the meaning of the dimensions, so the researcher must attempt to determine these either through supplementary research or by inferring them from the locations of the various drugs on each axis. For example, the researcher might be able to establish the horizontal dimension by posing the question: "What does Brand 1 have more (or less) of than Brands 5 and 3?" From his own knowledge or by asking questions of a few doctors he may discover it is something like "amount or severity of side effects."

Another way to identify these dimensions is from questions asked of doctors in the original survey. Thus, when a doctor says that Brands 1 and 5 are quite different, he might be asked, "In what ways are they different?" An analysis of these differences may provide additional clues to determine the meanings of the two axes. Or, each doctor might be asked to rate each brand on each of five to ten characteristics (e.g., severity of side effects); these ratings would help

Figure 3.1

TWO-DIMENSIONAL ORTHOGONAL MAP
FOR PHYSICIAN STUDY

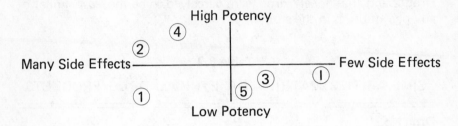

identify dimensions by showing what Brand 1 was rated high on that Brands 3 and 5 were rated low on.

In this study, interpretation of the axes suggested that the doctors differentiated among the brands primarily on the basis of their perceptions of both the level of potency and the number of side effects of each. The specific locations of brands on the map reveal how the panel of doctors *in aggregate* perceived each brand in relation to all others on the two dimensions. For example, Brand 1 was seen as having low potency and many side effects. Of course, doctors often differ in their perceptions of brands. While on the average the doctors saw Brand 1 as we just described, some doctors might have perceived it as *high* in potency or as having *few* side effects. This variability in customer perceptions of products offers segmentation opportunities if, for example, there is a sizable subgroup of physicians with similar perceptual maps that differ from those of the majority.

Individual Level Analysis

While there are several MDS approaches to studying individual differences in perceptual space for products under investigation, the best known is INDSCAL [3, p. 50]. This method first establishes a *single set of axes* for all members of a sample and then develops a *differential weighting of each axis for each respondent* in the sample. The weights (showing the relative importance of each axis or feature for each respondent) can be used to define the private perceptual space for each individual.

Market segments can be identified by finding groups of individuals who have similar sets of weights for each axis. These individuals are perceiving differences among products in a similar manner, so they may constitute a segment that can be appealed to by a special marketing mix.

Another form of individual level analysis that is superior to INDSCAL in some ways is "points of view" analysis. In this approach, respondents are first sorted into groups that are similar in terms of their direct similarities judgments (i.e., their similarities matrices); these groups are considered to have the same points of view with regard to the objects being scaled. Then a separate perceptual map is developed for each group.

The advantage of this approach is that different groups of respondents may have perceptual maps whos axes (i.e., salient features) are very different from those of other respondents. Yet INDSCAL would produce only a single map with a single set of axes. Points of view analysis permits entirely different axes for each of several perceptual maps [see 5].

The Ideal Product

Going back to the drug-mapping study, an individual doctor's choice from among the five brands depends not only on his perceptions of each brand, but also on his *preferences* for each level of each of the attributes. Since the perceptual map of ethical drugs was constructed solely from similarities judgments, it offers no specific information as to what kind of drug would be preferred by the most doctors—that is, what characteristics the "ideal" drug would have. Nonmetric scaling offers two major ways of dealing with respondent preference data: (1) models based on preference rankings only, and (2) models using either similarities or similarities-preferences data. The latter are more widely used and are of particular interest here, since we already have a similarities map of ethical drug brands (Figure 3.1) and are interested in locating the ideal drug somewhere in this configuration.

For some similarities maps the ideal product/service is obvious, since all axes represent inherently desirable features and respondents are almost certain to prefer a product/service having the most of these features (e.g., better taste and lower cost in a food product). For others, however, some form of trade-off may exist between the two principal features (axes), as in this case of drugs preferred by physicians. The sample of doctors in this study preferred (on average) a drug with medium potency and few side effects (labeled "I" on the map—the ideal brand).

As with perceptions, though, individuals' preferences may differ. Thus, some doctors may well believe that a *high* potency drug even with some moderate side effects would be ideal. This segment of doctors would have a different ideal point on the map. It is even possible that the most preferred product has some features other than those that constitute the axes of the perceptual map. That is to say, the preference map for a given product may have different dimensions than the similarities map for the same product. There is evidence that this is often the case [2, p. 89].

Determining the ideal product in the context of analyzing both similarities and preferences data simultaneously (joint space analysis) can be done by either of two principal approaches or models: *distance* and *vector*. The distance model implies that some *point* can be found within the similarities configuration that represents the ideal product—a single point in the case of all respondents combined, or several ideal points to reflect tastes of single individuals or of groups of individuals with similar tastes. The further away from this ideal point each object is, the less it is preferred; the closest is preferred above all others.

For the distance model the ideal point could be anywhere on the entire perceptual map. It would be on the perimeter in the case of products/brands where the two or three principal features (axes) are relatively independent and both or all are obviously desirable (e.g., friendliness and good food). It would be somewhere in the interior in cases where some optimum, rather than maximum, levels of attributes are desired (e.g., sweetness and carbonation in a soft drink, medium potency in a drug).

In contrast, the vector model assumes that an ideal product lies *somewhere on the perimeter of the similarities configuration,* so that a vector (arrow) from the origin can pass through this point. The farther out from the center one goes on this vector, the greater the preference for a product/brand; that is, the more of the two or three principal features a given product possesses, the more it will be preferred. The direction of the arrow indicates which of the two or three principal features is *most* important (i.e., whatever axis the arrow is closest to is most important in influencing preference). In reality, vector models are special cases of the distance model in which ideal points are assumed to extend to infinity.

It is possible, of course, to have a "mixed" model, with an ideal point on one dimension and a preference vector on the other. This might be found in the case of soft drinks, for example, where consumers would be looking for a drink that "tastes best" and has only moderate amounts of sugar or carbonation.

Perhaps the easiest way to deal with the problem of preferences is to include an "ideal product" as one of the products to be scaled (distance model). The respondent treats this as just another product and proceeds to compare it to all others as if it were a real product. The ideal product is thus included within the initial matrix of similarities, to be processed by the scaling algorithm. Note that this approach is based on similarities comparisons only and does not require the consideration of both similarities and preferences (joint space analysis). Green and Carmone point out several reasons why this may not be a feasible approach and offer as an alternative the PREFMAP model of Carroll and Chang, which considers both similarities and preferences using either distance or vector models, as the investigator chooses [2, p. 78].

The nonmetric version of vector models asks subjects simply to rank order all objects in terms of preference. The model then finds a vector (or set of vectors) such that the *order* of the *projections* of the objects to be scaled on the vector agrees as closely as possible to the original rank of preference given by the respondent. The angular direction of this vector shows the relative importance of the various features (axes) for the total sample or for a single individual.

Nonmetric Preference Mapping

All discussion of MDS thus far has centered on the development of *perceptual* positioning maps; the axes of the maps represent those features or attributes that people use to judge *similarities or differences* among competing products or services. These features *may or may not be the ones people want* most in a particular product or service class.

In contrast, *preference* maps have axes that purport to represent attributes that people want most in a given product/service category. There are two generic approaches to constructing preference maps:

- Internal analysis of preference data

- External analysis of preference data

Nonmetric scaling provides technologies for constructing both types of maps [see 3, Chaps. 4 and 5].

Internal analysis refers to the development of preference maps using only preference ("dominance") data—usually in the form of ranks. Respondents are asked simply to rank order their preferences for the various products/brands under study, and this matrix of ranks (product ranks x respondents) is processed using various nonmetric scaling algorithms. Some of these algorithms produce maps that represent respondents as vectors and products as points in a common space; others represent both respondents and products as points in a common space. The former are known as point-vector models, the latter as point-point models. Still other solutions produce a space that shows either respondents only or products only.

One difficulty with any such map is that of identifying or naming the vectors that serve as axes of the map. While this is true in the case of nonmetric *perceptual* maps, the problem is perhaps even more severe in the case of preference maps which, for example, may have *respondents* as "vectors" (axes) rather than product characteristics or attributes.

In contrast, *external analysis* preference maps are developed by fitting preference data into the stimulus spaces found from *prior* analyses of similarities data. These analyses of similarities matrices produce *perceptual* maps, and the process of locating ideal points or vectors within these maps was discussed earlier in this chapter.

Some Managerial Implications of Perceptual Mapping

Perceptual (and preference) mapping has proved to be of value to marketers who are attempting to develop and introduce new brands or to reposition existing ones. For example, consider the implications of the map developed from the doctors' perceptions and preferences for ethical drug brands (Figure 3.1):

Introducing new brands. Since there are no existing brands that are near the ideal or preferred brand (moderate potency, few side effects), a gap in the market seems to exist. A new brand approaching this combination of attributes might capture a sizable share of the market. Likewise, if different clusters of doctors have differing brand perceptions or attribute preferences, market segments may be identified to which new brands with specific attribute combinations might appeal.

34

Repositioning existing brands. Perceptual maps describe the way customers see brands at present. But marketers have the means to change customers' perceptions through new advertising, packaging, and the like. This objective can be achieved by repositioning one's own brand or by repositioning the competition (e.g., using comparative advertising).

A variety of reasons may motivate such a repositioning campaign. Specifically, one brand may be perceived as very similar on certain product dimensions to another in the company's line, resulting in cannibalization. For example, if Brands 3 and 5 (Figure 3.1) were offerings of one firm, an attempt to differentiate them by emphasizing the lesser side effects of 3 could result in expanded total sales.

Another repositioning strategy is recommended when customers "incorrectly" perceive a company's brand. For example, suppose laboratory testing reveals that Brand 1 is actually higher in potency than Brand 2, even though doctors perceive the reverse. If this misconception is detrimental to Brand 1, the firm may benefit by "correcting" the error through promotion efforts. In this regard, sometimes a firm's advertising tends, over a long period of time, to drift into misrepresenting a product by stressing the wrong features, by over- or underemphasis of certain features, or by displaying inappropriate types of people in the ad (the beer industry did this at one time when they showed their product being consumed by families of obviously high socioeconomic status). Perceptual mapping can be particularly useful in diagnosing and correcting problems of this kind.

Advantages and Limitations of Multidimensional Scaling

Nonmetric scaling methods have several rather specific advantages:

1. Many researchers feel it is much easier for respondents to rank order items (in terms of similarities and preferences) than to indicate their perceptions of "psychological distances" between objects in terms of units on some form of interval scale. They feel that respondents can more reliably give *ordinal* judgments, in the sense of being able to tell that one subjective magnitude exceeds or falls short of another—without being able to specify by how much.

2. The various computer algorithms (computation procedures) that develop perceptual maps from the rank-ordered inputs up-

grade the data from ordinal scales to interval scaled or better. Thus, initial ordinal psychological distances among objects are represented in terms of ratio-scaled spatial distances. (This occurs asymptotically as the number of objects to be scaled increases for a fixed number of output dimensions.)

3. The criteria respondents use to judge similarities among objects are not specified in advance. Each respondent is asked only how similar various objects or pairs of objects are, or to rank order his or her preferences for the objects, or for similar simple judgments. This is especially useful in situations where possible criteria are relatively obscure (e.g., in the case of comparisons among university curricula, among various types of business publications or institutions, or among different types of beverages or cleaning products), or where criteria are socially sensitive (e.g., personal hygiene products, items with strong social status connotations). In such cases it is often not clear what specific attributes or features should be rated.

4. *Nonmetric scaling emphasizes the close relationship of the final perceptual map to the original data inputs.* Most nonmetric computation procedures compare spatial relationships among objects *directly* with the initial data input matrix at every stage, and the final map is the one that best fits the original inputs from respondents. Other techniques which we will discuss later, do not do this to nearly the same extent.

5. "Nonmetric multidimensional scaling" is *not* restricted to nonmetric input data. Researchers will often ask subjects to judge the degree of similarity of one object to another on a seven- or ten point scale. These values, rather than ranks, become the entries in the similarities matrix, requiring slightly different computer algorithms for processing. This is not required, however; input can be in the form of the original rankings assigned by computers.

6. Nonmetric scaling (as well as metric scaling which will be discussed later) allows a points-of-view analysis, whereby respondents are grouped into segments that are homogeneous on the basis of their perceptions of (or preferences for) the competing products/services (i.e., their similarities matrices are very similar). Scaling can then be done within each segment separately, to portray more accurately the composition of the entire market.

36

On the other hand, nonmetric scaling also has some limitations:

1. Obtaining input data in the proper format can be a problem. The construction of a complete similarities matrix by each respondent is quite time consuming, especially when the number of objects to be compared exceeds eight to ten (although techniques for overcoming this are constantly being refined). The time required often precludes obtaining different kinds of useful information in the same field survey.

2. "Somewhat more troublesome is the fact that, even when the data *are* of a superficially appropriate form to be used as input for a particular multidimensional scaling method, this is no guarantee that they should be so used . . . . Worse still, the fact that just certain types of methods are readily available may lead an investigator to choose the kind of data he is going to collect solely on the basis that they be of the superficially correct format for one of those methods, without ever giving careful consideration to the question of what sort of data are most likely to provide a real insight into whatever phenomenon is under study." [2, p. 11]

3. There is also the problem that some rank-order data (such as those collected for nonmetric scaling) do not indicate *degrees of relationships* among objects being scaled. The objects scaled may all be quite similar, very dissimilar, or somewhere inbetween. This information is hidden by obtaining rankings from respondents initially.

4. Some observers feel that requiring individuals to rank order pairs of objects in terms of their overall similarities presents a task that is, at best, more difficult than rating these objects on attributes or characteristics, and, at worst, actually beyond the mental capabilities of many people. Since there is no direct evidence on this matter the question is moot. In any event, the task is quite difficult for many respondents.

5. Experience has shown that generally at least ten objects must be compared to produce two or more dimensions using MDS techniques; using fewer objects usually results in only a single-dimension solution. This is ordinarily not the case with the metric scaling techniques to be discussed in later chapters.

6. It is possible to have a set of objects (to be compared and scaled) that are so diffuse and dissimilar that no good common perceptual dimensions can be found by MDS. This is not a weakness of the MDS statistical technology; it is simply a reflection of the many different aspects of various dissimilar objects that must be considered by consumers when making direct comparisons among these objects. One of the current authors conducted a study involving direct comparisons between nine different types of sauces (e.g., mustard, catsup, relish, steak sauce, spaghetti sauce, thousand island dressing). It was not possible to find only two or three dimensions that would adequately reflect a common perceptual space for all the products. Respondents simply perceived these various sauces as being too different on an overall, "detached" point of view that did not consider either the types of foods the sauces would be used with or the physical product characteristics of each sauce.

Other advantages and disadvantages of MDS are discussed in an excellent manuscript by Ginter and Deutscher [1].

On balance, multidimensional scaling represents a powerful and versatile tool for studying perceptual and preference relationships of brands, products, services, and business firms. It has advantages that make it more appropriate for certain research needs than any of the other technologies. And it has a well-established track record in applications to both consumer and industrial markets.

REFERENCES TO CHAPTER 3

1. Ginter, James L. and Terry Deutscher. "Techniques for Generating a Multidimensional Perceptual Space: A Comparative Evaluation of Multidimensional Scaling and Discriminant Analysis," Paper Series WPS 76-25, College of Administrative Sciences Reprint and Working Paper Series, Ohio State University, April 1976.

2. Green, Paul E. and Frank J. Carmone. *Multidimensional Scaling and Related Techniques in Market Analyses.* Boston: Allyn & Bacon, 1970.

3. Green, Paul E. and Vithala R. Rao. *Applied Multidimensional Scaling.* New York: Holt, Reinhart & Winston, 1972.

4. Neidell, L. A. "The Use of Nonmetric Multidimensional Scaling in Marketing Analyses," *Journal of Marketing,* 33 (October 1969), 37-43.

5. Tucker, L. R. and S. Messick. "An Individual Differences Model for Multidimensional Scaling," *Psychometrika,* 28 (1963), 333-67.

OTHER REFERENCES FOR NONMETRIC SCALING

Clevenger, T., G. A. Lazier, and M. L. Clark. "Measurement of Corporate Images by Semantic Differential," *Journal of Marketing Research,* 2 (February 1965), 80-2.

Crespi, L. "Use of Scaling Techniques in Surveys," *Journal of Marketing,* 25 (July 1961), 69-72.

Day, R. L. "Systematic Paired Comparisons in Preference Analysis," *Journal of Marketing Research,* 2 (November 1965), 406-12.

Eastlock, J. O., Jr. "Consumer Flavor Preference Factors in Food Product Design," *Journal of Marketing Research,* 1 (February 1964), 38-42.

Green, P. E., F. J. Carmone, and P. J. Robinson. *Analysis of Marketing Behavior Using Nonmetric Scaling and Related Techniques.* Philadelphia: Marketing Science Institute, 1968.

Green, P. E. and D. S. Tull. *Research for Marketing Decisions,* 3rd ed. Englewood Cliffs, N.J.: Prentice-Hall, 1974, 222-9.

Richards, Elizabeth A. "A Commercial Application of Gutman Attitude Scaling Techniques," *Journal of Marketing,* 22 (October 1957), 166-73.

Shepard, Roger N., A. Kimball Romney, and Sara B. Nerlove. *Multidimensional Scaling: Theory and Applications in the Behavioral Sciences.* New York: Seminar Press, 1972.

Chapter 4

POSITIONING USING FACTOR ANALYSIS

In scientific endeavors it is often the case that there is more than one way to the promised land. So it was with positioning maps. As marketing scholars became more aware of the potential of this new development, they cast about for alternative technologies with which to construct such maps.

There were several reasons for this search for alternatives: (1) lack of time or interest to master the considerable complexities of nonmetric multidimensional scaling; (2) lack of readily available computer programs installed and operational at a particular working location; (3) reluctance to accept one or more aspects of the conceptual foundations of nonmetric scaling techniques; (4) conviction that this type of scaling did not fit certain research needs; and (5) preference for using classical and related statistical techniques that were both well understood and readily available.

One of the most obvious alternatives was factor analysis, a technique that was both widely understood and easily applied by most investigators. It was readily adaptable for multidimensional scaling purposes, even though it was not formally a part of that body of technology. Moreover, the output format was for all practical purposes indistinguishable. And, it required input data that were often more easily obtained and better understood by most market planners. Unfortunately, it also contained conceptual weaknesses that were not readily apparent even to many researchers, much less to operating marketing executives.

This chapter looks at some examples of positioning maps developed by factor analysis. Maps of this type are usually based on respondent ratings (perceptions) of several products or brands on each of perhaps 10 to 20 attributes or features. Factor analysis is performed on these ratings to extract the basic dimensions (factors), which then become the axes of the positioning map. Products or brands are each given a "score" (technically, a factor score) on each axis, reflecting the degree to which each product possesses each major feature. These are based directly on ratings given each product by respondents. The resulting map purports to be *interpretable* in exactly the same way as those produced by nonmetric scaling, even though it should not be interpreted the same since the two kinds of maps are seldom comparable.

Comparison of Factor Analytic and Nonmetric Scaling Techniques

While both nonmetric and factor analysis scaling start with a matrix of similarities, these similarities refer to very different things. For nonmetric scaling, entries reflect the perceived similarities among *objects* directly; for factor analysis, entries reflect the perceived similarities among the *attributes or features* used to rate the various objects. This explains why the two types of positioning maps can be quite different in terms of axis definitions.

Factor analysis groups together attributes or features that are seen as similar (i.e., are rated about the same) by respondents. The resulting groupings are merely descriptive adjectives that mean about the same thing to people; hence, *factor analysis simply performs an exercise in semantics* by identifying groups of similar statements. The size of each grouping depends only on the *number* of feature statements rated that are seen as similar and *how* similar they are seen to be. In turn, the number of similar statements that are included for a particular grouping depends only on the very arbitrary choice of the researcher. Therefore, it is literally true that the axes of a factor analytic positioning map can be determined *in advance of the analysis* simply by deciding how many statements about a given aspect of a product are to be rated by respondents.

The first factor extracted by factor analysis is always the largest grouping, and this becomes the first axis of the positioning map; the second grouping becomes the second axis, and so on. Yet these feature groupings may or may not have anything to do with either (1) the bases on which people perceive similarities or differences among products, or (2) features people want in a product. The resulting maps are usually all but useless for marketing planning purposes.

In making comparisons with nonmetric scaling, several other items are of interest. First, note that respondent judgments for factor analytic maps are initially obtained on *metric* scales, in the sense that each respondent rates each product usually on five-, seven-, or ten-point scales which are considered to have interval properties. Therefore, input data do not need to be "upgraded"—they are assumed to be metric (or near metric).

Proponents of nonmetric scaling object to metric scaling on three counts: (1) respondents may not be able to accurately rate similarities among items in terms of units on some adjective scale; (2) even though these units appear equal they may not in fact reflect equal psychological distances (i.e., interval scales) in the minds of respondents; and (3) since the basic similarities matrix used to construct the positioning map must be *derived* from respondent ratings of *attributes* using factor analysis, respondents should be asked to construct their own similarities matrix *directly* by making comparisons between pairs of the *objects* to be scaled, as is done in nonmetric scaling.

There is also the problem of selecting features or attributes to be rated. There is never any real assurance that all features that are most important to the consumer have been selected for rating, since no systematic procedure exists for determining the relative importance of all features *prior* to a positioning study. If one or more key features were omitted this would never be known. There are additional problems with factor analytic scaling that will be discussed at the end of this chapter.

Nonetheless, factor analysis can be defended on grounds that it is a legitimate data-reduction technique for finding the basic dimensions underlying a group of attributes that characterize objects under investigation. Whether the results are meaningful from a market planning standpoint is another matter.

Product positioning based on factor analysis is illustrated below, using a study of snack foods conducted by one of the authors. Two different approaches and maps will be shown: the first using factor analysis in the usual way, the second using a modified technique known as weighted covariance analysis.

FACTOR ANALYTIC MAP OF SNACK FOODS

Scenario

The case study reported here involves snack foods served to children by mothers in the Los Angeles area. Almost any competitive situation involving several products or brands, either consumer or industrial, could have been chosen for study. Snack foods were selected because the use of these foods has grown rapidly in recent years, and especially because of the great differences among foods in terms of characteristics and desirability. Such products tend to make meaningful analysis more difficult using conventional techniques, and they should serve as a good showcase for the different types of positioning maps.

A convenience sample of 150 mothers was asked to rate each of ten snack foods on each of fourteen features or characteristics: filling, fattening, juicy, complexion, messy, expensive, teeth, oily, energy, easy to eat, nourishing, stains, easy to serve, and child likes. The snack foods selected for study were: apples, oranges, raisins, milk (whole), ice cream, potato/corn chips, peanut butter sandwiches, snack crackers, candy, and cookies. Mothers were asked for the following information:

1. Ratings of each food on each characteristic, on a seven-point scale

2. Frequency of serving each food *as a snack* for their children age twelve or under

3. Importance to the mother of each of the fourteen characteristics in terms of choosing a snack food to serve (hereafter called "stated importance")

4. Selected additional information on demographics, family weight, eating habits, and diet factors

Interviewers were instructed to locate 150 mothers of different ages and races in selected locations throughout Los Angeles. For purposes of this study, sample characteristics were not considered important, since the objective of the study was to show methodology and approach and not to accurately portray the market situation. Therefore, study results may not apply to the general public nationwide, or even in Los Angeles.

Developing the Dimensions

To review, statistical product positioning requires two ingredients:

1. A set of axes or dimensions which represent the principal groups of features considered by respondents to be most important in perceiving or evaluating products

2. Spatial location of each product in terms of these principal features

Conventional factor analysis could have been used to analyze snack food ratings on the fourteen features, to develop groupings of similar features that could serve as dimensions (axes) for the positioning map. There are, however, several problems with this approach, as we discussed earlier.

Another, perhaps less objectional, approach is to factor analyze the *importance ratings* given each feature by each mother. Assuming respondents really know the importance of each feature to them and are telling the truth, these ratings at least tell us what mothers feel influences them the most in choosing among competing snack foods; this might be more useful for decision-making purposes. Note, however, that this would still produce a "semantic" space rather than either a perceptual or a preference space.

For the present study, it was determined that the principal dimensions used to position the ten products should be those features that mothers consider most important in deciding whether or not to serve a particular snack food to their children. Therefore, the data analyzed consisted of each mother's ratings on a four-point scale of how important each feature was to her in deciding whether or not to serve a particular snack food to her children (extremely important, very important, etc.). Factor analysis of these ratings produced two major groupings of features: nutrition and convenience. Factor loadings (which "define" the factors) are shown in Table 4.1.

This table indicates that mothers who felt "nutrition" was important in a snack food also tended to feel the food should be "good for teeth," "good for complexion," and "not oily." Similarly, those who felt the snack should be "easy to serve" also felt it should be "easy to eat out of hand," "should not stain," and should be "not messy." These groupings were used as axes for the positioning map.

Table 4.1

FACTOR LOADINGS FOR FOURTEEN FEATURES: FACTOR ANALYSIS OF STATED IMPORTANCE RATINGS

Characteristics	Factor Loadings for Dimension I	II	Mean Importance Rating
1. Filling/not filling	.317	.073	2.90
2. Fattening/not fattening	.424	-.009	2.64
3. Juicy/dry	.301	.125	3.28
4. Bad/good for complexion	.645	.104	2.19
5. Messy/not messy to eat	.204	.664	2.67
6. Expensive/inexpensive	.244	.347	2.43
7. Good/bad for teeth	.762	.056	1.53
8. Oily/not oily	.516	.240	2.65
9. Gives/doesn't give energy	.541	.165	2.21
10. Easy/hard to eat out of hand	-.069	.796	2.83
11. Nourishing/not nourishing	.565	.116	1.70
12. Stains/doesn't stain clothing, furniture	.250	.664	2.55
13. Easy/hard to serve	.046	.747	2.87
14. My children like it/ dislike it	.071	.243	1.86

Scale: 1=extremely important; 2=very important; 3=fairly important; 4=of little importance.

Spatial Representation

To locate each of the ten products in relation to each of the two axes, a score was developed for each product on each axis; this score represents a weighted summation of the ratings given by mothers to each of the separate features that go into making up each dimension. For example, the convenience dimension reflects ease of serving, ease of eating the food out of hand, and food that does not stain. For each mother it was necessary only to add together her weighted ratings on each of these features for each product separately, to develop an average score reflecting how convenient (or nutritious) the mother felt a particular snack food was. These scores were plotted to obtain the spatial configuration shown in Figure 4.1.

Looking left to right along the horizontal (nutrition) axis, we see that most foods at the left side appear to be less nutritious, while those at the right side (milk, apples, oranges) are clearly nutritious. Looking up and down the vertical axis, raisins are perceived to be the most convenient food, followed closely by apples, snack crackers, and cookies, while ice cream is perceived to be by far the least convenient. The latter probably reflects the effort required by the mother to get the ice cream out of the freezer, scoop it into a dish, and produce a spoon; that the child must wrestle with both spoon and dish in eating the ice cream; and the various clean-up efforts.

It would seem, then, that the spatial configuration makes sense in terms of the snack foods used for this study.

Figure 4.1

POSITIONING MAP FOR SNACK FOODS: CONVENTIONAL FACTOR ANALYSIS USED

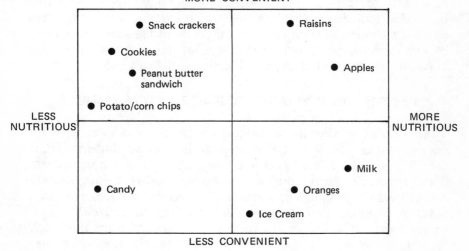

Ideal Snack Food

Location of the ideal point—the most desirable food—on the map is a puzzling matter. There is serious question that it can or should be done at all for a semantic map. The primary problem is that the axes of the map may or may not have anything to do with either perceptual discrimination or preference evaluation. Thus, it is questionable that *any* ideal point on a semantic map would be actionable from a market planning standpoint.

If for some reason we wanted to locate an ideal point in terms of semantic space, this would best be accomplished by the vector model (discussed in Chapter 3) rather than by including an "ideal snack food" as one of the items to be rated. This is because the ideal snack would probably be rated at the extreme end for most of the fourteen features (mothers would want as much as possible of each feature), which would distort correlations among features as well as the extraction of factors as axes for the map. Thus, such an approach would not be technically feasible.

At a more pragmatic level, discussions so far in this book have dealt with finding *the* ideal point within any given type of positioning map. It is likely, however, that there are several ideal points for any product type. This is not only because different people want different things (i.e., market segments), but also because the same person often wants different products for different situations or occasions. In the case of snack foods, a mother might want one particular snack food for days when the child is indoors, another for days when the child is outside. Some mothers like to serve a wide variety of snacks to their children no matter what the occasion. All of this makes the problem of ideal-point location a difficult one.

FACTOR ANALYSIS OF WEIGHTED COVARIANCES

A modified version of factor analysis can be used to construct a *preference map,* using matric ratings of product attributes as input data. We consider this method to be far superior to the more conventional approach presented above, primarily because it does not rely on respondents' "stated importance" ratings for each of the attributes or features. This new technique is known as *weighted covariance analysis;* it is demonstrated below using data from the snack food study, so the reader can easily make comparisons with the conventional approach.

Generally speaking, construction of positioning maps by factor analyzing respondent ratings on several attributes or features has two major weaknesses in addition to those discussed above:

48

1. Factor analysis produces vectors or axes by looking for groups of attributes that are similar in meaning to the respondent: for example, nutritious, good for teeth, good for complexion in the case of snack foods. This means that even features that are *most* important in determining choice behavior would certainly be overlooked *if they were relatively independent of other features being rated;* that is, they would not statistically group with other features and therefore would not emerge as a "factor."

2. Similarly, size or importance of a dimension extracted by factor analysis is based only on *how many* other features are judged to be similar and *how similar* these other features are—the more that are similar, the greater the apparent "importance" of the vector or axis. It might caustically be observed that if degree of importance of factors extracted in conventional factor analysis turned out to be the same as their actual importance in influencing choice decisions, it would be only by accident!

To overcome these limitations, Forgy and Myers developed a modification of the conventional factor analytic approach [1]. Rather than factor analyzing *correlations* among features or attributes, they proposed analyzing a matrix of *covariances* among features; these covariances are weighted in terms of the importance of each feature in determining choice among products or brands. This procedure overcomes both of the problems discussed above, and it produces a *preference map* that is considered by the present authors to be much more useful than either the semantic map based on "stated importance" ratings of features or any kind of perceptual map.

Factor analysis of weighted covariances first develops a matrix of covariances[1] for all attributes rated. These covariances are then "stretched" to reveal the differential importance of each attribute. Stretching is done by multiplying the covariances in each row (and corresponding columns) by "importance" weights for that feature.[2]

---

[1] Covariance formula: $\dfrac{\Sigma xy}{N}$ (deviations from respective means)

Correlation formula: $\dfrac{\Sigma xy}{NS_x S_y}$

[2] These importance weights consist of the "B" coefficients from the multiple regression of all rated attributes versus overall evaluation or a similar criterion measure. For the snack food study, the criterion was frequency of serving each food.

The reader may wonder why the importance of each feature could not be established more simply by using stated importance ratings obtained directly from mothers. Previous research has shown clearly that there are major differences between the features people *say* are important and how strongly the same features *relate to frequency of use* of a product [see 3]. In the absence of definitive evidence as to which measure is more accurate, the authors prefer regression weights since they are more closely related to actual behavior, as reported by respondents.

Multiplying row/column covariances by importance weights increases the variance of each attribute in proportion to the importance of that attribute (as measured by its correlation with frequency of use). Since factor analysis extracts factors in the order of the amount of the total variance each one explains, a factor can be extracted even if it consists of only a *single* attribute or feature. And, factors will be extracted in order on the basis of how they relate to the relative frequency of serving all types of snack foods. *Hence,*

Figure 4.2

POSITIONING MAP FOR SNACK FOODS:
WEIGHTED COVARIANCE FACTOR ANALYSIS USED

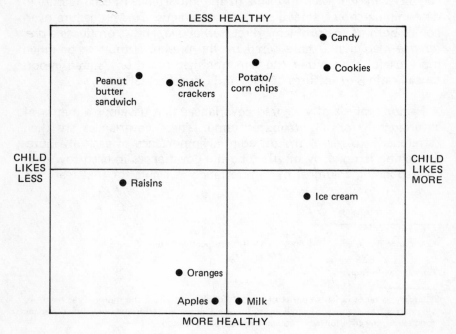

products can be positioned in terms of features having the greatest relationship to frequency of serving snack foods.

Snack Food Covariance Analysis

Applying weighted covariance analysis to the original ratings of snack foods by 150 mothers produced the factor loadings shown in Table 4.2 for the first two factors. Scores for each snack food on these factors produced the configuration shown in Figure 4.2. Note the great differences from Figure 4.1, which used conventional factor analysis. One of the axes (nutrition) has remained, but the other (convenience) has been replaced by a new dimension, "child likes."

Table 4.2

FACTOR LOADINGS FOR FOURTEEN FEATURES: WEIGHTED COVARIANCE FACTOR ANALYSIS OF SNACK FOOD RATINGS

Characteristic	Factor Loadings for Dimension	
	I	II
1. Filling/not filling	.047	.008
2. Fattening/not fattening	-.089	-.778
3. Juicy/dry	-.005	1.066
4. Bad/good for complexion	-.007	-.168
5. Messy/not messy to eat	-.001	.004
6. Expensive/inexpensive	-.001	-.005
7. Good/bad for teeth	.127	1.613
8. Oily/not oily	.020	-.585
9. Gives/doesn't give energy	-.027	.260
10. Easy/hard to eat out of hand	-.074	-.261
11. Nourishing/not nourishing	-.003	.082
12. Stains/doesn't stain clothing, furniture	-.009	-.050
13. Easy/hard to serve	-.023	.004
14. My children like/dislike it	4.763	-.474

Conventional factor analysis of stated importance ratings, reported earlier, showed that nutrition was the largest dimension; in contrast, weighted covariance analysis indicates the even greater importance of how much the child likes a particular snack food, since this feature showed the highest correlation with frequency of use. Nutrition is of only secondary importance, while convenience is a weak third. *How well children like a particular snack food should clearly be the axis of primary importance in the preference map.* As it turned out, "child likes" was an isolate feature—not related to any others—so it *could not* have emerged using conventional factor analysis.

Nonlinear relationships present special problems. Sometimes people prefer some moderate rather than maximum level of a particular attribute, such as sweetness or carbonation in the case of soft drinks. Usually a suitable mathematical transformation function can be found to produce a straight-line relationship for such an attribute. Or, an ideal point can be located on the axis at the point of maximum preference, based on a simple scatterplot of the attribute with overall preference or choice.

Weighted covariance analysis has been used very successfully for such other product categories as small cars, motorcycles, beverages, and table sauces. The authors feel it offers considerable promise as a positioning technique. It seems particularly appropriate for well-established product lines, where the objective of the market planner is to identify a gap in present product offerings that gives promise for a new entry. It is less appropriate when competing offerings and/or product attributes or features are not as well understood (e.g., weighing different types of recreation or travel against spending the same dollars for home furnishings and appliances, or the introduction of some entirely new type of food product). In such cases nonmetric scaling (Chapter 3) or benefit structure analysis (Chapter 8) would normally be more appropriate.

Factor Analysis of Preference Ranks

Factor analysis of weighted covariances is not the only way to construct a preference map. Some investigators ask respondents simply to rank order each product/service in terms of overall desirability, and then they factor analyze correlations among these ranks. The resulting factors constitute the axes of the map, which is based entirely on preferences rather than perceptions.

This approach is a useful "quick and dirty" method. Compared to most other scaling approaches, the required input data are extremely easy to secure from respondents. There is, of course, some question whether metric factor analysis should be used on rank-order correlations, but nonmetric factor analytic techniques are also available. Factor analysis of preference ranks is most useful when the investigator wants a relatively quick and inexpensive map of consumer "preference space" for well-defined product categories. It has the disadvantage of not dealing with ratings of features or attributes, so interpretation of axes may be difficult.

Note that both factor analysis of weighted covariances and factor analysis of ranks produce *preference* maps, as opposed to perceptual or semantic maps. Besides the greater potential relevance of the former for many market planning purposes, there is the added advantage of not having to be concerned with ideal points or vectors. Preference maps by their nature have directional axes, so the more of a particular attribute or feature the better. But *the researcher must make sure that significant curvilinear relationships do not exist,* as when consumers want some moderate amount of a particular feature rather than the maximum amount (e.g., sweetness, carbonation).

Advantages and Limitations

Factor analysis of weighted covariances has several attractive features as compared to nonmetric scaling:

1. Ratings of products or services on various attributes are more likely to be familiar and well understood by both respondents and market planners. The latter do not have to *infer* identities of the major dimensions (axes) of perceptual maps based on spatial configurations of objects, as in most nonmetric scaling approaches. Thus, there is less feeling of reliance on "black box" technology.

2. Data are initially obtained on metric (interval) scales—at least these scales probably have more interval than ordinal properties. This enables the determination of *amounts or degrees of relationships among attributes or products,* in contrast to the ordinal relationships which reflect ranks only.

3. Factor analysis of weighted covariances makes a serious effort to overcome two weaknesses of conventional factor analysis:

(1) it attempts to weight important features more heavily than others (based on their correlation with some independent criterion of desirability), so that axes of perceptual maps will reflect the most *relevant* attributes or features used by consumers to evaluate a product or service; and (2) product features that are quite important but are very independent of other features can become one of the axes of a perceptual map when weighted covariances are used, whereas factor analysis of correlations would not select any important features that are relatively independent.

4. Weighted covariance analysis uses familiar and readily available computer programs: factor analysis and multiple regression, for the most part. Weighting programs can be developed without too much difficulty.

Of course, weighted covariance analysis also has some weaknesses:

1. Correlation is not causation. There is no assurance that importance weights using "B" coefficients from multiple regression accurately reflect the true influence of a particular feature. Other means of determining importance would include experimentation (usually costly and often totally impossible) and asking respondents to *rate* importance on a scale. The latter approach is suspect, however, in view of findings from other investigations [see 3].

2. Careful preliminary work must be done (e.g., focus group interviews) to insure that product attributes rated by respondents include all features that have a major influence on preference or choice behavior. This would not be a problem in nonmetric scaling but it could be a serious one in weighted covariance mapping. For example, the most important feature in the snack food study (child likes) could easily have been overlooked as being too obvious. The investigator has the responsibility for ensuring inclusion of *all* relevant features. There are two problems in this connection: (1) there are no formal or quantitative tests for spotting omissions; and (2) including all potentially important attributes can involve a very long list, making rating a great burden for respondents. (A prior factor analysis of ratings on a separate sample can reduce the number of attributes, but this means extra time and expense.)

3. Initial ratings assume that respondents can make meaningful judgments on interval scales, which nonmetric scaling advocates doubt.

4. Even if respondents are asked to rate only five to ten objects on ten to fifteen attributes, this represents a considerable investment of time and cost, with attendant possibilities of respondent fatigue. The problem can be overcome to some extent by asking each respondent to rate only two or three objects, but this involves the assumption of equality of subgroups (probably tenable if care is taken).

On balance, factor analysis of weighted covariances has a legitimate place alongside other positioning approaches. It can be very useful if done with careful preparation and thoughtful interpretation. However, positioning maps based on *conventional* factor analysis are not recommended by the present authors.

For an excellent comparison of factor analysis with MDS technologies (in Chapter 3) see MacCallum [2].

REFERENCES TO CHAPTER 4

1. Forgy, Edward W. and James H. Myers. "Preference Mapping Using Weighted Covariance Analysis," working paper, 1976.

2. MacCallum, Robert C. "Relations between Factor Analysis and Multidimensional Scaling," *Psychological Bulletin,* 81 (1974), 505-16.

3. Myers, James H., and Jonathon Gutman. "Validating Multi-Attribute Attitude Models," in Ronald C. Curhan, ed. 1974, *Proceedings of the American Marketing Association.* Chicago: 1975.

Chapter 5

POSITIONING USING
DISCRIMINANT ANALYSIS

Another approach to product positioning has been suggested by Johnson [3]. He proposes applying discriminant analysis to product/ service attribute ratings to establish the perceptual space for products of a given type.

Discriminant analysis is a technique used to distinguish or discriminate among items or groups of some kind (e.g., products, brands, people, firms) on the basis of measurements or ratings on a number of attributes that can be used to characterize these items. The basic premise for positioning by discriminant analysis is similar to that for nonmetric scaling of object *similarities* data: *the greater the perceived difference among objects on a particular feature, the more important that feature is in establishing the perceptual space for these objects.*

In constructing a positioning map, the items to be distinguished among are the competing products or brands of interest, and the attributes are the product characteristics rated by respondents. The technique develops *discriminant functions,* which consist of a single attribute or a grouping of similar attributes that distinguish best among *all* the items rated by respondents. Since these discriminant functions can be represented as a vector in space, they can be used as axes of a *perceptual* map. Several of these functions may be required to characterize consumers' perceptual space, and the positioning map is drawn using the first two or three of these as axes.

Products/services are positioned on each axis on the basis of their average ratings on that axis. These averages are obtained by entering average values on each attribute for each object into each of the first two or three discriminant function equations in turn. (This is readily accessible from the output of most available computer programs.)

The approach uses input data identical in format to that used for factor analysis: respondent ratings of several products on five- to ten-point scales for each of several features. However, the objectives of discriminant analysis are very different from those of any type of factor analysis, so results are usually quite different even though they are displayed the same.

Rather than presenting an example of perceptual mapping by discriminant analysis using a published study, we feel it will be more instructive to apply this technique to the same snack food data presented in Chapter 4. This allows easy comparison of three *metric* positioning techniques: ordinary factor analysis, factor analysis of weighted covariances, and discriminant analysis.

DISCRIMINANT ANALYSIS MAP OF SNACK FOODS

In applying discriminant analysis to the snack food study, the objects to be discriminated among are the ten snack foods. Since each food was rated on each of fourteen product characteristics, each food constitutes a "group" in fourteen-dimensional space. The problem is to find the two or three discriminant functions that best identify the major differences among foods (i.e., that best separate the groups in space). These functions become the axes of the perceptual map.

Each food was designated a separate group and all ratings were entered into an available computer program.[1] Coefficients of the first three discriminant function equations are shown in Table 5.1. Entries are the coefficients for each characteristic, showing roughly the *relative importance of that characteristic in defining each discriminant function.* The largest coefficients indicate characteristics that are most important in separating the groups, that is, features that are the most *different* between groups.

---

[1] BMD 07M, BMD Biomedical Computer Programs, W. J. Dixon, ed., University of California, Berkeley, 1967.

Table 5.1

DISCRIMINANT COEFFICIENTS FOR TWO DIMENSIONS

	Dimension	
Characteristic	I	II
Not filling	-.01	.00
Fattening	-.09	.26
Juicy	.50	.36
Bad for complexion	-.13	.18
Not messy to eat	.03	-.11
Expensive	.03	.01
Good for teeth	.18	-.15
Oily	-.18	-.06
Gives energy	-.01	.11
Easy to eat out of hand	-.11	-.22
Nourishing	.20	-.17
Stains	.00	.09
Easy to serve	-.03	.04
My children dislike	.06	-.25
Cum. Prop. of total dispersion of group means	.61	.78

The first perceptual dimension is defined at one end by foods that are juicy (.50), nourishing (.20), and good for teeth (.18); and at the other end by not oily (-.18), not bad for complexion (-.13), not easy to eat out of hand (-.11), and not fattening (-.09). This appears somewhat similar to the "nutritions" dimension established by both conventional factor analysis and factor analysis of weighted covariances. However, since the largest coefficient by far here is "juicy," it is difficult to determine the clear identity of this first discriminant function. There is no particular reason why nourishing foods *should* be any more or less juicy than any other kind, although this tended to be the case for some of the snack foods selected for this study. In any event, the first dimension is somewhat obscure—is it juiciness or nutrition? If juiciness, what relevance does this have for market planning?

The second dimension too, is characterized at one extreme by foods that are juicy (.36) but that are also fattening (.26) and bad for complexion (.18); and is characterized at the other extreme by my children dislike it (-.25),[2] easy to eat out of hand (-.22), nourishing (-.17), and good for teeth (-.15). This is probably the "child likes" dimension found by factor analysis of weighted covariances. As in the case of the first function, however, the identity of this second factor is not really clear.

Coefficients for each dimension were applied to average ratings for each snack food on each characteristic; the resulting averages were plotted for the first two dimensions, as shown in Figure 5.1. This configuration is somewhat different from either of the two previous positioning maps, as would be expected, but it seems to be more similar to the "weighted covariances" map than to the one for ordinary factor analysis. This is in spite of the fact that the discriminant analysis map is a *perceptual* map, while weighted covariances produced a

Figure 5.1

POSITIONING MAP FOR SNACK FOODS:
MULTIPLE DISCRIMINANT ANALYSIS USED

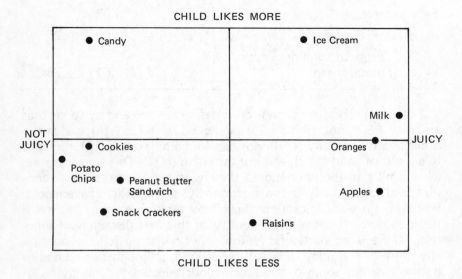

_____

[2]The negative sign here means that the factor is *not* characterized by children disliking it; hence, children *do* like it. Similarly, this factor represents foods that are *not* easy to eat out of hand, *not* nourishing, and *not* good for teeth.

preference map. However, the axes of the discriminant map do not appear to be as clearly defined as those for the weighted covariances map. In summary, the reader must judge for himself which of the three positioning maps produced the most "reasonable" configuration and would be most useful for market planning purposes.

Ideal Point Determination

"Ideal" products are normally located within the discriminant perceptual space in one of three ways:

1. By a *vector* of rank-order preferences for the objects, similar to that used by nonmetric scaling researchers; this consists of the average preference rank for each object for the entire sample.

2. "By deducing the number of ideal points at each region in space by using data on whether a product has too much or too little of each attribute. This procedure has not yet been fully explored, but at present seems to be appropriate to the multidimensional case only when strong assumptions about the shape of the ideal point distribution are given." [3, p. 16]

3. By having each respondent rate his or her own ideal product on the same attribute scales used for existing products. This approach has distinct limitations for most types of products, however; often many features rated are intrinsically desirable (e.g., durability, good taste), and respondents tend to rate their ideal product at the highest extreme on each attribute scale. For example, in rating service stations most people want the greatest possible speed, friendliness, quality of products, convenient locations, and so on, at the lowest possible price. In other cases, such as food or beverage products, respondents have difficulty conceptualizing an "ideal product" (e.g., could people who now relish Coca-Cola have accurately described such a drink on attribute scales *before* it was first developed and offered?) Still, an ideal product rating may sometimes be feasible.

Thus, the ideal product can be displayed either as a point or as a vector, the same as for nonmetric scaling or for conventional factor analysis. Each investigator must select the alternative most appropriate for the particular type of product/service under study.

Comparisons among Scaling Techniques

Note that three of the major techniques presented up to this point (nonmetric scaling, ordinary factor analysis, discriminant analysis) normally have the twin objectives of: (1) establishing the *perceptual space* for a group of objects based on, (2) *similarities* (or dissimilarities) of some sort.

For nonmetric scaling, similarities are based on direct comparisons among the *objects* to be rated; these can be measured either nonmetrically (ranks) or metrically (interval scales). For factor analysis, the similarities are in terms of correlations among the *attribute or feature scales* on which several products/services are rated. For discriminant analysis, similarities are in terms of *dissimilarities or contrasts among the objects* as reflected by differences in their ratings on the same types of attributes as in factor analysis.

In contrast, factor analysis of weighted covariances does not develop a perceptual space but rather produces a preference space. Axes are not based on perceived similarities among either objects or attributes; rather they are based on the "relative importance" of the various features on which the products/services are rated. This importance is established by correlations of attribute ratings with some measure of overall evaluation of the objects rated. Nonmetric scaling can also be used to establish preference maps [see 2], although most published work to date has presented perceptual maps based on direct similarities judgments.

The issue of the comparative usefulness of perceptual versus preference maps cannot be disposed of easily. Indeed, the objectives of the study and the nature of the objects or issues to be positioned should always dictate the choice of approaches. The present authors feel that preference maps will usually be more useful in the normal situation where brands or products compete head-on. From the market planner's standpoint, it is probably more meaningful to present maps whose axes represent the major features or characteristics of a product/service consumers consider most important in *evaluating* competing alternatives. Objects can then be positioned in relation to these axes, in two- or three-dimensional space.

On the other hand, the planner sometimes needs to know how people will *perceive* a product in relation to others on the market. Is Carnation's Breakfast Bar perceived as a breakfast food or as a nutritious snack good any time of day? Would a picante sauce be perceived as just another kind of Mexican sauce or would it also compete against steak sauce, mustard, and the like? A perceptual map would probably be more useful for problems of this type.

ADVANTAGES AND LIMITATIONS OF DISCRIMINANT ANALYSIS

Discriminant analysis has certain advantages and limitations as compared to other positioning approaches. Among the advantages are:

1. It is probably the best technique for developing a *perceptual* map when metric ratings of product characteristics on interval scales are desired. There is the assumption, of course, that perceptual space is based on perceived similarities and differences among products/services being evaluated: the greater the perceived difference among objects on a given feature, the more important that feature is in establishing a perceptual space.

2. Discriminant analysis develops axes for the perceptual map in sequential order, starting with the feature or group of similar features that best distinguish among the products/services being evaluated. The relative importance (size) of each discriminant function is given in quantitative terms.

3. In contrast to ordinary factor analysis, discriminant analysis does not require *groups* of similar features to establish an axis: a single "isolate" feature will be selected if it discriminates better among objects than any of the groupings.

4. This technique provides statistical tests of significance of the differences among *all* objects, to show the extent to which all products/services differ in perceptual space. It also provides such a test for the difference (perceptual distance) between any two products.

5. Practitioners feel that another advantage of discriminant analysis is that it requires only that a given respondent rate a *single* product/service on each of the various features. Since often 10 to 20 features are rated, respondent fatigue in evaluating 5 to 10 objects on each feature can be considerable. (On the other hand, this same rating procedure could be used for both types

of factor analytic approaches; ratings could be pooled across all respondents to produce a single correlation or covariance matrix, which could then be processed as described in Chapter 4. This requires the same assumption of equivalence among respondent groups made in discriminant analysis, but it is usually a reasonable assumption.)

6. "Unlike nonmetric procedures, distances estimated among a collection of products do not depend upon whether or not additional products are included in the analysis. Any of the brands . . . could have been deleted and the remaining object locations would have had the same relationships to one another and to the attribute vectors." [3, p. 16]

Given that the objective is to establish a perceptual space among products based on metric ratings, discriminant analysis is a very useful technique. On the other hand, this technique does have disadvantages, many of which are common to any approach to developing *perceptual* maps using *metric* inputs:

1. Respondents may not be able to evaluate product/service attributes on an interval scale, as nonmetric scaling proponents contend.

2. There is never any real assurance that all the most important attributes have been included for rating. Any failure of discriminant analysis (or factor or weighted covariance analysis) to provide a clear and meaningful perceptual space could mean either that there are not in fact any major differences among the groups (products/brands) *or* that some of the most important distinguishing attributes have been left out. Preliminary focus group or in-depth interviews are probably the best insurance against this latter problem.

3. Discriminant analysis makes the assumption that the attributes or features rated have a linear relationship to one another; it also assumes that the "dispersion matrix" (covariances between attribute ratings) is the same for each product. These assumptions are usually reasonable for the normal competitive situation.

4. Some features of a product or service may not be perceived to differ to any meaningful extent among existing competing

brands; for example, safety of money deposited in banks, safety of household appliances. These features would not emerge as axes of a discriminant map; thus, they could easily be overlooked in designing new products and services. Yet any offering that was *not* perceived as safe by consumers would surely fail.

This latter point is a problem common to all perceptual maps which focus on the major *differences* among competing products or services. These maps *appear* to represent to the market planner (even though they may not actually do so) that:

1. Features that do not distinguish much among existing offerings are of little importance.

2. The more a particular feature distinguishes among existing offerings, the more important it is for new product and promotion planning purposes.

Neither of these assumptions may be true.

In regard to the latter point, Shocker and Srinivasan note,

It is questionable whether seeking weighted combinations of attributes that discriminate "best" among brands is an objective appropriate to determining a configuration of products useful in analyzing preferences, since there need be no logical relation between the weights estimated for the attributes that define the dimensions of such a space and those attributes relevant to preference decision making. [4, p. 924]

To illustrate this point, a study of the small-car market in the U.S. by one of the present authors found that gas mileage showed greater perceived differences among cars than any other feature rated; yet gas mileage ratings correlated only weakly with respondents' overall evaluations of the eight cars rated (this was prior to the oil embargo). In contrast, a feature showing relatively small-rated differences among cars was found to correlate by far the most highly with overall evaluations of the cars. A *perceptual* map would have shown gas mileage to be the most important dimension, while a *preference* map would have shown it to be third most important. In fact, the rank order of importance of the three most important features[3] for small cars was *inversely* related to the perceived differences among the cars on these three attributes in this particular study!

---

[3]Based on correlations of each feature against overall evaluations of the cars, pooled across all cars and all respondents.

As another illustration, banks may be perceived to differ widely in size. But how *important* is size in choosing among competing banks? And which are preferred: large, intermediate, or small neighborhood banks?

All of this points to *the need for market planners to understand clearly the differences between perceptual and preference positioning maps and to know what each is based on.* There is no "best" map—each type is better suited for some planning needs than for others. The choice must be made in advance by the planner with consultation by the researcher.

For additional points of comparison between multidimensional scaling technology and discriminant analysis, the reader is referred to an excellent article by Ginter and Deutscher [1].

REFERENCES TO CHAPTER 5

1. Ginter, James L. and Terry Deutscher. "Techniques for Generating a Multidimensional Perceptual Space: A Comparative Evaluation of Multidimensional Scaling and Discriminant Analysis, " Administrative Sciences Working Paper Series WPS 76-25, Ohio State University, April 1976.

2. Green, Paul E. and Vithala R. Rao. *Applied Multidimensional Scaling.* New York: Holt, Rinehart & Winston, 1972.

3. Johnson, Richard M. "Market Segmentation: A Strategic Management Tool," *Journal of Marketing Research,* 8 (February 1971), 13-18.

4. Shocker, A. D. and V. Srinivasan. "A Consumer Based Methodology for the Identification of New Product Ideas," *Management Science,* 20 (February 1974), 921-37.

Chapter 6

MARKET SEGMENTATION USING MULTIVARIATE ANALYSIS

The term *market segment* refers to *subgroups of consumers who will respond in a similar manner to a given marketing mix.* The problem is how to identify groupings of consumers in such a way that they will actually respond differently to different market mixes.[1] There are two principal approaches to locating useful market segments: (1) *a priori* and (2) response based.

A priori segmentation designates groups of consumers who are similar in terms of some factor or factors that are known or felt in advance to be related to product/service consumption; for example, demographics, psychographics, heavy versus light usage, brand loyalty. In contrast, response-based segmentation looks for *patterns* of product usage, attitudes, perceptions, and the like, that might hopefully signal useful market segments.

In this chapter we are interested only in the latter approach to segmentation. We are not interested in *a priori,* single-factor segmentation based on seasoned judgment or previous research; usually this approach is univariate (one variable at a time). Rather, we will be concerned with response-based segmentation which involves multivariate analysis—the consideration of many variables simultaneously.

---

[1] In practice, the term *market segment* is often used to refer to groups of people who are similar in ways *not* related to market response [see 2].

68

Ideally, multivariate response-based segmentation research is a three-step process:

1. *Identifying* groups of respondents who are similar in terms of their patterns of response to some portion(s) of a survey questionnaire (e.g., usage rates, product benefits wanted, perceptions of or preferences for competing products/brands, usage patterns)

2. *Describing* these segments in terms of demographics, psychographics, and other information

3. *Validating* findings using field research, to see if the identified segments do indeed respond differently to a given marketing mix

This chapter concerns itself with the first of these steps—identification of potential market segments based on patterns of information contained in survey questionnaires. Several appropriate statistical methods for identifying these groups of respondents are discussed below.

Types of Segmentation

Wilkie has proposed a conceptual framework for classifying the wide variety of approaches to market segmentation [11]. He sees all contemporary segmentation research as falling into one of two categories: "Empirical Stream" and "Product Stream."

The Empirical Stream includes most of the published studies dealing with quantitative segmentation efforts. It is based primarily on the microeconomic theory of price discrimination, which defines segments whose demand schedules differ with respect to price and promotion. These segments are *first* defined in terms of readily available demographic and/or psychographic data; then their product usage rates are compared. Or, the market is segmented on the basis of product usage rates, and then demographics, psychographics, and media habits are used as descriptors.

In contrast, the Product Stream approach analyzes brand choice and perceived differences within a product class, and emphasizes specific brand evaluations and purchases *of the individual,* rather than total product class purchases. Segments are thus related to both the person *and* the product and not to the person alone (as in the Empirical Stream).

To paraphrase, Product Stream segments are defined by patterns of what a person *perceives* and *does* in relation to a product rather than by his or her own demographic or psychographic characteristics or by usage rates. Examples of Product Stream segmentation include product positioning by market segment, segmentation by similarity of perceptions, segmentation by similarity of usage patterns, and segmentation by product features or characteristics considered most important in purchasing decisions.

This chapter will deal primarily with Product Stream segmentation but will expand Wilkie's definition to include segmentation based on *responses to any kind of survey questionnaire item.* Some of these items may relate to patterns of brand choice or usage; others may elicit perceptions of products or brands; still others may relate to a variety of other topics such as activity patterns and assorted attitudes, opinions, and behavior of the respondent. Current Product Stream segmentation research is generally based on multivariate statistical techniques that identify clusters or groups of respondents who have similar patterns of response to questionnaire items.

Segmentation versus Structure

A mistake that inexperienced researchers sometimes make in segmentation research is that of finding groups of similar survey *responses* rather than *respondents.* For example, one survey asked subjects to indicate what types of merchandise (e.g., clothing, appliances, furniture, kitchen items, garden and other tools) they usually bought at a particular department store. The objective was to see if there were patterns among items bought; for example, do people who buy, say, appliances at this store also buy other hard goods but not soft goods and decorative items? This involved a clustering of *responses* to the various items (using R-type factor analysis).

Three groupings of merchandise purchase patterns were found—call them A, B, and C. Type A included three related types of merchandise such that when one of these was purchased by a given respondent he or she also tended to purchase others in that grouping. *Note that these are not market segments,* only clusters of goods that are similar in terms of purchasing patterns. Such an analysis provides a type of market "structure" that is often helpful in understanding a given market even though it does not identify groups of *respondents* (i.e., segments) that are similar in terms of purchasing patterns.

However, the relationship between groupings of responses and potential segments of respondents is a very direct one. If there are k groupings of responses, there are 2^k possible market segments. In the example above, the three clusters of merchandise lead to a possible eight groupings of respondents, since these are all the possible combinations of buying (or not buying) A, B, and C: that is, A but not B or C, B but not A or C, and so on. This shows why it is usually much easier to find *clearly understandable market structure by searching for groupings of responses rather than respondents:* there are always many more potential groupings of the latter.

It should thus be clear that the search for market structure does not always lead to the identification of market segments, in the true sense of that word. Segmentation is only one form of market structure, and it may or may not be the most useful form for a given market planning objective. Unfortunately, careless usage of the term by some marketers has tended to obscure its real meaning and to group all attempts at market structure under the rubric "segmentation."

Procedures for Identifying Market Segments

There are several appropriate statistical techniques for identifying market segments. These techniques search for groupings of objects (people, in this case) that are similar in terms of some set of descriptor variables (e.g., benefits wanted, perceptions, usage patterns, etc.). The objective is to search for "natural groupings" of objects that show the "order" among all the objects being measured. In segmentation research, clearly defined natural groupings of people are considered to be market segments.

Once groupings have been identified, it is usually important to describe the inhabitants using descriptors *other* than those used to establish the groups. Discriminant analysis is an effective technique for this purpose; it develops a profile of each segment in terms of various descriptors (e.g., demographics, psychographics) so that each group can be better understood.

(Discriminant analysis also performs another function that is sometimes useful, more so in other fields [e.g., medical diagnosis, entomology, botany] than in marketing. Whenever natural groupings

71

have already been established for a given data set using grouping or clustering techniques, there is sometimes the problem of deciding which grouping some "new" case falls into. This is the problem of "classification," a process that is complementary to that of "clustering." Discriminant analysis develops a scoring formula [discriminant "function"] that characterizes each *a priori* grouping; then each new case is scored by each of the scoring formula, and the resulting scores are used to decide in which grouping the new case most likely belongs.)

In practice, grouping or clustering is one of the most difficult statistical analyses to implement, for several reasons:

1. The investigator never knows in advance *how many* natural groupings there are in the data or, indeed, if there are any at all! Nor is there any generally accepted statistical test for determining this with precision.

2. Once some arbitrary number of groupings (segments) has been decided on, there remains the problem of determining which respondents belong in each. This is solved by some investigators by assigning *every* respondent to the "nearest" grouping, so that all respondents are classified. Usually, however, this approach results in diluting the composition of each group or segment to the point where it is not markedly different from the others; hence, its identity becomes obscure. The present authors feel this approach should generally be avoided.

   Some professionals find that often only 50 percent to 75 percent of all respondents belong *clearly* to *any* of the groupings that are established. This is a consequence of both the great inherent variability among human beings and the variability among the items used as a basis for the grouping.

3. Selection of the items to be used as a basis for the grouping is strictly arbitrary, yet the choice will greatly affect the kinds and numbers of groups that are found. For example, should respondents be grouped on the basis of benefits wanted? Perceptions? Usage patterns? Or some combination of these? Or all of these? *In general, the more heterogeneous the types of items used to group respondents are, the less likelihood there is of finding any meaningful segments at all.*

Thus, it would ordinarily be better to group respondents separately on the basis of, say, product image rating and then, say, patterns of products used than to combine both sets of responses into the same segmentation analysis.

4. While a wide variety of techniques have been developed, not many of these are readily available or well understood. Nor is the basis for choosing among these as clear as for many other types of statistical techniques. Considerable experience is required to select the best techniques for a given objective and a given body of data.

Some insight into the problems of clustering or grouping can be gained by looking at Figure 6.1. Using data from the snack food

Figure 6.1

PLOT OF IMPORTANCE OF CONVENIENCE
AND NUTRITION IN CHOICE OF SNACK FOOD

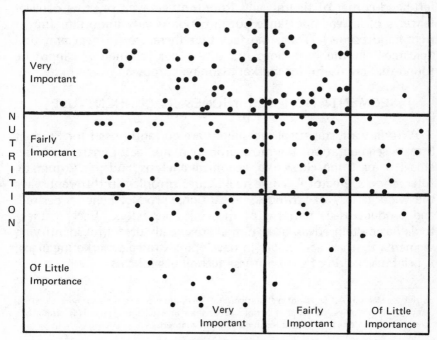

study discussed in earlier chapters, this figure contains a plot showing how important mothers felt each of two product features—nutrition and convenience—was in determining what snack foods to serve to their children. Each entry on the plot represents an individual mother whose sum of ratings was averaged across three statements relating to nutrition (or convenience).

The objective of clustering to find *natural groupings* of respondents that are close to one another but are clearly separated from other natural groupings by plenty of white space; that is, to find groupings that not only do not overlap but that are not even contiguous. Simple inspection of Figure 6.1 shows that no such natural groups exist. (In technical terminology, there are no "modes" in the data; hence, no good clear clusters.) Does this mean that there are no actionable segments? Not necessarily.

The upper left-hand corner of this figure contains many mothers who say that *both* nutrition and convenience are *very* important. These mothers are clearly different from those who say that nutrition is of little importance but convenience is very important (lower left-hand corner of figure), and from mothers who say that convenience is of lesser importance but nutrition is very important (upper right-hand corner). Thus, the fact that there are no neat and tidy "clusters" in the data does not mean that "segments" cannot be found that are useful for market planning purposes.

SEGMENTATION TECHNIQUES IN CURRENT USE

A variety of statistical techniques are currently used for Product Stream segmentation; the most prominent are factor analysis, hierarchical or partition clustering, canonical analysis, and the Automatic Interaction Detector.[2] These techniques organize in different ways the wide variety of attitudes, perceptions, product benefits desired, and product usage patterns of the consumer public. Each of these tools has certain advantages; not all are equally useful for identifying segments that are *actionable* in developing strategic marketing plans. A brief discussion of each of these techniques follows.[3]

---

[2]Strictly speaking, A.I.D. is not a "multivariate" technique, since each step consists of examining all variables, but one at a time rather than simultaneously; nor is it primarily a clustering technique in the strict technical sense of that term.

[3]Multiple regression, discriminant analysis, and multidimensional scaling are not included here because none is primarily a grouping or clustering technique.

Factor Analysis

Factor analysis may be used to find groups of either similar *responses* or similar *respondents*. It was pointed out earlier that similar patterns of responses do not constitute market segments; it is groupings of similar respondents that we are interested in. "Inverse" factor analysis (Q-type) is the appropriate technique for segmentation purposes. This approach is used to group respondents in terms of responses to a specified subset of questions in a survey.

Strictly speaking, factor analysis is *not* a "clustering" or "grouping" technique; it is designed for "data reduction"—for finding a small number of basic dimensions or factors underlying a set of observed measurements. Still, this technique is widely used by marketing researchers for segmentation purposes for perhaps three primary reasons:

1. Computer program "packages" for factors analysis are widely available.

2. This technique is well understood by most researchers.

3. Factor analysis does produce groupings of items (respondents) that are similar in composition; generally speaking these groupings would not be greatly different from those produced by the more appropriate but often more complex clustering techniques discussed below.

For these reasons factor analysis is not inappropriate for segmentation purposes, and it is certain to continue to be used widely in the future. There is, however, at least one major caveat of a technical nature. It might happen that two segments of a total population are "mirror opposites" of one another. For example, one segment might want a soft drink that is sweet and highly carbonated; another might want the opposite—a sour drink with very low carbonation. Or, one segment of shoppers might buy furniture, clothing, and other decorative items but not appliances at a particular department store; the other segment might have the opposite purchasing pattern. In such cases factor analysis would pull both segments together into a single "factor," with high positive loadings for one segment and high negative loadings for the other. The researcher must inspect his results carefully for evidence of this phenomenon.

75

Another problem with factor analysis is nontechnical: computer time (and therefore cost) goes up as the *square* of the number of variables being analyzed. In a segmentation study the "variables" are people; hence, costs increase as the square of the number of people analyzed. For segmentation purposes it is important to have a large number of subjects initially so that any clusters found will have enough cases to make each cluster sufficiently stable to enable meaningful comparison between the clusters in terms of descriptor variables. This usually means a minimum of perhaps 150 to 200 people.

Even this number of subjects will be rather costly, but costs go up rapidly as the number approaches 500 (not uncommon for a segmentation study). Costs for 1,000 or more people become intolerable for all but the largest business firms (if, indeed, a suitable computer and/or program can be located at all). There are ways around this problem,[4] of course, but they result in multistage processes that are not as satisfying as if all respondents had been used initially.

Green and Tull suggest that one of the best approaches to segmentation using factor analysis would be to first do a principal components analysis (similar to R-type factor analysis) of the response variables that are to be used as a basis for grouping; this would reduce the number of variables that go into the grouping procedure by eliminating overlap. The result is a "reduced space" consisting only of those few factors that are the basic dimensions underlying the set of original variables (questionnaire items). Then, segments can be formed using *all* of the original variables, and these segments would be embedded in the reduced space. "This dual approach, if the dimensionality is small, enables the analyst to stay 'close to his data' and possibly to augment the clustering results with visual inspection of the configuration." [7, p. 446]

Clustering Methods

From a technical standpoint, the *most* appropriate tools for finding groups of similar respondents are known as clustering techniques. The two most widely used clustering techniques are:[5]

---

[4]For example, use factor analysis to find groups among a subsample of 200 respondents, classifying the remaining respondents into the "best" cluster using discriminant analysis or some other suitable technique.

[5]Neither of the two approaches is really suited to accomplish another hoped-for result from clustering methods: to detect whether there are any "natural" groupings (i.e., multiple modes) in the data [4]. Investigators often seem to believe that they have found such. However, both clustering techniques will usually suggest "natural" groups just as clearly when applied to *artificial* samples of populations of the same dimensionality *but known to have only a single mode*—for instance, a joint normal pupulation. Unfortunately, there is no generally effective solution for this very interesting problem.

1. Hierarchical clustering

2. Partition (or threshold) clustering

Various algorithms exist for each of these, as indicated below.

Hierarchical Clustering. Hierarchical clustering methods are often used by researchers seeking market segments. These methods normally develop clusters in a stepwise fashion, joining items (people) that are most similar to one another, then adding items into the clusters formed in previous steps, and proceeding in this fashion throughout the entire set of items to be clustered. Final output is in the form of a "dendrogram" (tree) showing which items were joined first and which items were added to each cluster in each step, with the final step having all items joined into a single massive "cluster" [see 9, 10].

This technique is illustrated in Figure 6.2 using adjectives describing hair shampoos rather than people (to better illustrate how hierarchical clustering joins items that are easily seen as similar). Items (words) that are most similar (in meaning) are grouped together first; then stray items are included in these primary groupings, followed by the joining of groups, and so on to the single final cluster. Note that the first step joins "body" and "fullness," the next step joins "natural" and "clean," then "curly" and "alive," and so on. As the items are grouped, the computer rearranges their locations so that similar items and clusters are listed together for convenience of interpretation. For each step, the computer indicates the "dissimilarity level" at which the grouping takes place. The scale for this is shown at the bottom of Figure 6.2.

While hierarchical clustering is a widely used and very acceptable clustering technique, it has at least one major technical flaw: namely, clusters formed at the later sequential clustering steps are usually not the "best" (i.e., most homogeneous) groupings of the items that *could* be formed at that clustering step [4]. For example, Step 10 in some clustering study may have produced three clusters with different numbers of cases in each. Usually the partitioning methods discussed below will produce three *more homogeneous groups,* with tighter fit, than hierarchical clustering. This is because hierarchical Step 10 cannot undo any of the four clusters already formed by Step 9; it can only join two of them. Put more intuitively, the best way to divide a pie into thirds is not by joining two of the quarters! So, typ-

Figure 6.2

HIERARCHICAL STRUCTURE OF 19-ELEMENT WORD ASSOCIATIONS (HAIR SHAMPOOS)

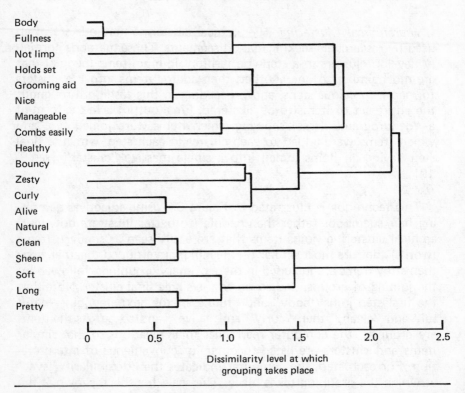

Dissimilarity level at which
grouping takes place

Source: Green, Paul E., Yoram Wind, and Arun K. Jain. "Analyzing Free-Response Data in Marketing Research," *Journal of Marketing Research,* 10 (February 1973), 45-52.

ically, hierarchical clusters are not nearly as tight as those that could have been formed *if it were known in advance how many clusters were needed.*

There is also the problem of interpreting hierarchical clustering results when searching for segments. Note that the dendrogram in Figure 6.2 provides both a new *number* and a new *configuration* of segments at each step. At what "level" does the researcher find the "proper" number of segments? While this question has no precise answer for any of the other clustering methods either, it is usually much harder to answer for hierarchical clustering since no clear "groups" are found at *any* stage in the process.

The present writers feel that while hierarchical clustering is technically suitable for quantitative segmentation purposes, other techniques are usually superior from either a technical or a managerial standpoint or both.

Partition Clustering. Partition clustering methods start the clustering process by specifying in advance how many clusters are to be formed. Even though the researcher cannot know this with any degree of certainty, he or she would ordinarily select some number between, say, two and six for segmentation studies. While more than five or six clusters might in fact exist, the market planner would not ordinarily have the resources to either *understand* each one thoroughly or to *plan* and *implement* a marketing mix for each; also, larger numbers of segments often would not each represent large enough markets for profitable marketing campaigns. From a technical standpoint, however, partition clustering can be done for any desired number of clusters [see 7, Chap. 13].

"Optimal partition" clustering begins by selecting as many starting points as there are groups desired, say, five. Five individuals are selected by some method (even at random) to form the initial "centroids" (center points), and "partitions" are drawn around these trial centroids to include all cases that are closer to each of these centroids than to any other centroid. These partitions form the initial segment configurations.

Because the initial centroid points are seldom the best that could have been selected as a center point for each of the five segments desired, the clustering algorithm selects a new centroid for each group (by calculating a sort of "center of gravity" for each initial cluster), repartitions, selects new centroids, repartitions, and so on until the best fit is achieved.[6] While the very best partitioning may still not be obtained from a given start, the result is almost always superior to the corresponding hierarchical groupings. Additional assurance of obtaining a very good partition can come from using several independent random starts.

---

[6]Maximum between group variance and minimum within group variance.

79

Since, as discussed earlier, the investigator does not usually know how many clusters he really has, it is necessary to specify in advance several different numbers of clusters desired, then to form each number using the iterative algorithm, and to develop some index of "fit" for each cluster (such as the sum of squared deviations of all terms from their respective centroids). Graphing the sum of squared deviations for successive numbers of groupings provides some insight into the number of clusters that seems most reasonable. (Another approach to determining the number of clusters that exist in a given body of data has been presented elsewhere [5].)

The soft drink example in Figure 6.3 shows how optimal partition clustering might partition a two-dimensional space containing the configuration of points shown here. Each point represents one respondent. Simple visual inspection suggests that there are three clusters (segments) of respondents. If the vertical axis represents the amount of carbonation wanted in a soft drink and the horizontal axis represents the amount of sweetness desired, respondents in Segment I want high carbonation and low sweetness, those in Segment III want the reverse, while those in Segment II want a very sweet drink with moderate carbonation.

Of course, as the number of dimensions (product features) increases, the possibility of finding segments that are so clearly delineated decreases. When the number of dimensions approaches ten to fifteen, there becomes less and less chance of finding any meaningful segments at all *unless* differential importance weights can be assigned to the various dimensions—to reflect the fact that some product features are much more important than others. Even then there are no known clustering techniques that could use such information in the search process for finding clusters. Thus, it is often the case that a researcher should first determine the three to six dimensions (product features) that have the greatest relevance for the total sample of respondents and then cluster respondents according to these key features only.

In summary, either of these two major clustering approaches is usually superior to factor analysis as a tool for market segmentation. Hierarchical clustering will better show *how* various items combine in terms of their similarities, while optimal partition methods will usually produce more homogeneous groupings for any given number of clusters. The investigator can choose one or the other, depending on his own objectives plus prior knowledge about the subject matter he is working with.

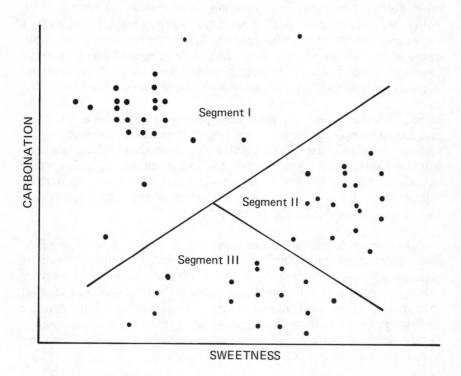

Figure 6.3

OPTIMAL PARTITIONING OF SOFT DRINK CLUSTERS

Automatic Interaction Detector

Both multiple regression and the automatic interaction detector (A.I.D.) are primarily tools for Empirical Stream research, but the groups produced by A.I.D. make it particularly useful for marketers looking for segments that are actionable. *Both techniques start with a single dependent variable* representing the primary thing of concern to the marketer (e.g., amount of product usage, buying intention, strength of preference for a brand or product) and proceed to systematically search through independent variables for those characteristics that relate most highly to variations in the dependent variable. Both stepwise regression and A.I.D. identify the single most important predictor variable first, then the next most important, and so on in turn until no additional variable will improve on prediction accuracy.

81

While the two techniques have similar objectives, they differ in the manner in which they handle the independent variables and in their underlying assumptions. Regression normally assumes *linear* relationships of independent variables with the dependent variable (as well as with each other) plus interval-scale independent variables, while A.I.D. assumes neither. Even if both assumptions can be met, so that regression can be used, the output on A.I.D. is intuitively much more easily grasped than regression. A.I.D. visually depicts *how* the various segments are constituted. It does, however, lack some of the statistical precision and stability of results found in regression [see 3].

Each method implicitly assumes a particular structure in the data, and it is an empirical matter as to which more closely corresponds to reality. If variables are measured on an interval scale and the relationships are linear and additive, then the regression equation is certain to predict better. On the other hand, if variables are qualitative or relationships are very nonlinear or nonadditive, then the tree-like segments created by A.I.D. should do better.

An example of segmentation using A.I.D. is shown in Figure 6.4. The objective of this investigation was to identify the factors that were most highly related to *length of decision time* for consumer purchases of major household appliances. Factors studied included information about both old products and new replacements, sources of information about products, other appliances and cars bought recently, selected demographics, future financial expectations, and the like. A total of 32 predictor items were studied.

Figure 6.4 shows the A.I.D. "tree" for purchase decision time. The amount of time between first thoughts of buying and actual purchase is the dependent variable, the thing to be predicted or understood. Items showing the greatest relationships are shown in the boxes from left to right.

The first "split" (most important predictor item) was degree of satisfaction with old product. Satisfied users averaged 14.18 weeks decision time; dissatisfied users, 23.15 weeks. There were 366 respondents in the former group, 273 in the latter. The next most predictive item for *satisfied* former users was *type* of appliance purchased; respondents buying a black-and-white TV, a washing machine, or an air conditioner averaged 9.15 weeks of decision time; those buying a car, a color TV, a refrigerator, or a stove averaged 16.60 weeks, and so on. Other splits are analyzed in a similar manner.

Figure 6.4

A.I.D. TREE FOR PURCHASE DECISION TIME

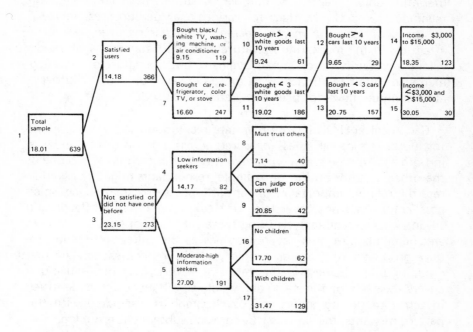

Mean decision time in weeks appears in lower left-hand corner and number of households in lower right-hand corner of each box. "White goods" are refrigerator, freezer, washing machine, or stove.

Note! For another similar illustration, see Newman, Joseph W. and Richard Staelin. "Prepurchase Information Seeking for New Cars and Major Household Appliances," *Journal of Marketing Research,* 9 (August 1972), 249-57.

Each box in Figure 6.4 is a market segment, consisting of all respondents with the indicated combination of characteristics. Each segment is identified as to the length of decision time, so comparisons are easily made. Of course, as the various splits proceed, the number of respondents in each segment becomes smaller, hence more unstable. This points out one caveat of an A.I.D.-type analysis: after the first split or two the resulting segments are so small and have been selected so precisely that they often *substantially overestimate the ability of the independent variables to predict the dependent variable.* A.I.D. normally overestimates to a much greater extent than regression techniques [see 3].

Canonical Analysis

Canonical analysis was introduced into the marketing research literature only recently. A number of studies have employed this technique to good advantage for various analytic purposes; however, its use *as a tool for market segmentation* has received very little attention in the marketing literature [see 6]. Canonical analysis develops a certain type of market segment, but the nature of these segments and their relationships to those derived from other multivariate techniques have not been adequately discussed.

Canonical analysis is a multivariate technique that can relate two (or more) *sets* of variables, measured across a group of respondents, in both a *clustering* and a *predictive* way. Other techniques do one or the other, but not both. For example, respondents might be asked to rate the relative importance of various aspects of a steak sauce: spiciness, color, does not cover taste of steak, aroma, natural flavor, and so on. A canonical analysis using these ratings as one set of variables and demographics plus psychographics as the other set would produce groupings of features people want in a steak sauce. The first grouping might be described in terms of features as a thick sauce that covers the taste of the steak, and would simultaneously be identified in terms of demographics and psychographics associated with this pattern of wants; the same is true for each subsequent grouping.

Hotelling has shown that canonical analysis is the equivalent of performing independent (principal components) analyses on each of the two sets of variables and then rotating the resulting component structures to develop weights for each variable which produce maximal correlations between components on each side [8]. In this way, a set of dependent variables can be related to a set of independent variables in a single operation to produce pairs of linear functions, each of which is maximally correlated with the other. This is repeated in such a way that each function is independent (uncorrelated) with the preceding functions on the same side. Each pair is called a "canonical variate" and is described by both the weights for each variable and the degree of relationship between the two functions. An excellent article by Alpert and Peterson has discussed the knotty problems of interpreting results of canonical analysis [1].

Usefulness of Canonical Analysis. The major question about the usefulness of this technique is: Can the canonical variates that emerge be regarded as market segments in the conventional sense? And, if so, how do these segments differ from those using other multivariate techniques? The answer has both a technical and a managerial side.

From a technical standpoint, the "segments" identified by each canonical variate:

1. Are not segments at all in the sense of being *groups of people* who have a similar pattern of response to questionnaire items

2. Are merely groupings of response patterns similar to those from the A.I.D. analysis of types of goods purchased from the department store (R-type factor analysis) discussed earlier in this chapter

3. Emerge *only* because they are predictable by (i.e., associated with) some linear combination of demographic, psychographic, and other descriptive items that a questionnaire happens to contain

Thus, patterns of responses that emerge as a canonical variate may not have *any* relationship to those that emerge from a clustering of product-use responses alone. It could thus be argued that it is better to search for response patterns independent of descriptive items to avoid overlooking meaningful market structure.

On the other hand, from a managerial standpoint the planner wants market structure that is "actionable," that he can "do something about" in his planning activities. Response structure from a set of variables such as volumes of products used, patterns of product usage, patterns of product characteristics considered important, and the like, is most useful to him to the extent that he can *describe* these patterns in terms of variables such as demographics, psychographics, or media usage. Without this, he is often at a loss to know how to reach certain people effectively.

Thus, whatever "segments" emerge in the form of canonical variates would seem at first glance to be exactly what the market planner wants. Each variate links a pattern of responses to various items of the questionnaire with some pattern of demographic, psychographic, media, or other variables to provide a form of useful market structure.

Looking at both technical and managerial aspects, one may say that canonical analysis *can* provide meaningful market structure—something the marketing planner can "do something about" because he knows "people characteristics" associated with a certain *response pattern.* On the other hand, it may be that some other response patterns are more frequent, better defined, and more meaningful, but they will not emerge in canonical analysis simply because of the particular selection of demographic and other characteristic variables included in the questionnaire. To the extent that an investigator has an effect on brand or product selection in the product lines he is interested in, *and* to the extent that he can include all of these factors in the questionnaire, canonical analysis may be a very useful tool for market *structure* purposes, even though it is not actually a bona fide technique for market *segmentation.*

Canonical Analysis of Snack Food Data. The same snack food data analyzed in earlier chapters was entered into a canonical analysis program, to allow comparisons of these results with those from other techniques. Usage rates of the ten snack foods served as one set of variables, and various descriptor items (demographics, diet habits, etc.) comprised the other set. Analysis of these sets produced the canonical variates and regression coefficients shown in Table 6.1.

Looking first at Canonical Variate A, one sees a vastly different pattern among the snack food usage set of variables from that found using the other multivariate techniques. Highest loadings are on whole milk (.66) and ice cream (.45), with no other food exceeding .20.

From a marketing strategy standpoint, Canonical Variate A seems to have actionable components. Mothers who serve both milk and ice cream: tend to serve all snacks more frequently, are younger, have children closer to ten to twelve years of age than four to six years of age. Evidently these women became mothers at slightly younger ages than other women in the sample, which is supported by their generally lower educational levels. On the other hand, none of the other information in the descriptor set of variables (e.g., family meal habits, diet habits, family weight characteristics) seems related in any meaningful way to whole milk and ice cream usage.

Canonical Variate B is more of an enigma, consisting of mothers who serve potato/corn chips but *not* snack crackers or whole milk to their children. The most characteristic descriptors are: older children,

Table 6.1

CANONICAL REGRESSION COEFFICIENTS (STANDARDIZED)

	Canonical Variate		
Item	A	B	C
Canonical correlation	.62	.55	.48
Percent of variance explained	.38	.30	.23
Potato/corn chips	.07	-.58	-.35
Whole milk	-.66	.43	-.65
Candy	-.09	.12	.22
Cookies	-.15	.25	.25
Apples	-.09	.14	.25
Peanut butter sandwich	-.20	-.27	.41
Raisins	-.02	.31	-.22
Ice cream	-.45	-.29	.24
Snack crackers	.06	.65	.35
Oranges	-.05	-.20	.09
Dinner together?	-.30	-.28	-.46
Breakfast together?	-.04	.00	.01
Child's weight	.35	-.11	.11
Mother's weight	.05	-.05	.40
Frequency of serving snacks	-.58	.37	.41
Children on diet?	.09	.04	.10
Mother on a diet?	.03	-.13	.57
Mother works?	-.06	.24	-.47
Mother's age	-.52	.33	.03
Education	-.33	.03	-.22
No. children at home	-.11	-.30	-.08
Child's age	.66	.72	-.32
Child's sex	.08	-.11	.19
Social class index	.14	.10	.15
Family income	.02	.37	.49

mother serves snack foods less frequently, mother slightly older, somewhat higher family income. Canonical Variate C links whole milk and peanut butter sandwiches inversely with: family usually dines together, mother seldom goes on a diet, mother employed full time, higher family income.

As compared with results from other techniques, usage patterns developed from canonical analysis seem so capricious as to make one wonder if they have any basis in fact at all, or at least if they are stable and meaningful enough to be useful for market planning purposes. This is in spite of the fact that all clearly meet the criteria of statistical significance ($p \leq .05$). From a planning standpoint, the manager wonders which "segment," if any, he should concentrate on since all are defined with almost equal clarity. Canonical Variate A probably has more mothers than the other two, but there is no way of estimating their proportion of the total number of mothers in the study.

DISCUSSION

The purpose of this chapter has been to point out the principal multivariate techniques currently being used for segmentation purposes and to show the more important differences among them. In choosing among the alternatives discussed here, the investigator must be guided by several considerations: (1) assumptions, data input requirements, and output of the various techniques; (2) nature of the raw data; and (3) needs and objectives of the market planner. It is evident from this discussion that market segmentation by multivariate analysis is not a simple problem with a single path to its solution.

REFERENCES TO CHAPTER 6

1. Alpert, Mark I. and Robert A. Peterson. "On the Interpretation of Canonical Analysis," *Journal of Marketing Research,* 9 (May 1972), 187-92.

2. Blattberg, Robert C. and Subrata K. Sen. "Market Segmentation Using Models of Multidimensional Purchasing Behavoir," *Journal of Marketing,* 38 (October 1974), 17-28.

3. Doyle, Peter and Ian Fenwick. "The Pitfalls of A.I.D. Analysis," *Journal of Marketing Research,* 12 (November 1975), 414-25.

4. Forgy, Edward W. "Cluster Analysis of Multivariate Data: Efficiency vs. Interpretability of Classifications," Paper presented at Biometric Society (WNAR) meetings, University of California, Riverside, June 22, 1965. Abstracted in *Biometrics,* 21 (September 1965), 768.

5. Fortier, J. J. and H. Solomon. "Clustering Procedures," in P.R. Krishnaiak, ed., *Multivariate Analysis.* New York: Academic Press, 1966.

6. Frank, Ronald E. and Charles Strain. "A Segmentation Research Design Using Consumer Panel Data," *Journal of Marketing Research,* 9 (November 1972), 385-90.

7. Green, Paul E. and Donald S. Tull. *Research for Marketing Decisions,* 3rd ed. Englewood Cliffs, N.J.: Prentice-Hall, 1970.

8. Hotelling, Harold. "The Most Predictable Criterion," *Journal of Educational Psychology,* 26 (February 1935), 139-42.

9. Johnson, Stephen C. "Hierarchical Clustering Schemes," *Psychometrika,* 32 (September 1967), 241-54.

10. Ward, Joe H., Jr. "Hierarchical Groupings to Optimize an Objective Function," *Journal of the American Statistical Association,* 58 (March 1963), 236-44.

11. Wilkie, William L. "Market Segmentation Research: A Conceptual Analysis," Paper No. 324, Institute for Research in the Behavioral, Economic and Management Sciences, Purdue University, September 1971.

Chapter 7

MARKET STRUCTURE STUDIES:
THE STEFFLRE PROCESS

In the early 1960s, while product positioning using various kinds of multidimensional scaling techniques was still in its infancy, a very different approach to new product planning was proposed by Stefflre. A cultural anthropologist by profession, Stefflre looked at product perception and product positioning in a manner very different from that of the statisticians and psychometricians then working in this area. He states:

> My own academic research interest lies in the study of relations between language and thought and/or language and behavior. In pursuing this topic I became interested in the role of the language spoken by members of a culture in influencing the way in which they behave toward specific new objects or events, and in the problem of the development and design of new items (objects or events) that when introduced into a selected culture elicit the desired patterns of beliefs and behavior from members of that community. [1, p. 1]

Stefflre used the beer bottle as an illustration of how differently various cultures throughout the world might perceive and use the *same object*, depending on such factors as cultural patterns, values, and language structure. Throughout most of the civilized world the beer bottle serves primarily as a container for beer. Yet one primitive culture might use it primarily as a weapon, another as a decorative object, another as a building material, and so on. This underscores the notion that few items have such clear *intrinsic* properties that they are likely to be used in only one way by all cultures. It therefore becomes of paramount importance to study the way in which certain items, or classes of items, are perceived, used, and described by a given culture.

90

This problem is a recurring one for consumer products companies that attempt to export a product that is successful in the United States into a foreign culture: members of that culture often perceive the product quite differently from U.S. citizens. One example is instant breakfast, which was introduced into Europe as a competitor for the normal breakfast fare. Since many Europeans prefer a filling, "hearty" breakfast, instant breakfast did not do well until it was repositioned as a quick meal for "emergencies." (The number of European "emergencies" subsequently rose rapidly!) This problem is an important one within the realm of new product development as well, which is where Stefflre chose to concentrate his investigations.

Stefflre's objective was to develop a *sequence* or *process* for designing and pretesting new products, objects, or ideas that would improve the probability of their success when introduced into a culture for the first time. This might have been done in any of several contexts: introducing technological innovation (new seeds, tools, practices) to increase economic productivity; introducing new governmental institutions, roles, or alternatives; or introducing new products or services to the consumer market.

Stefflre chose the new consumer product introduction setting because it met several criteria: (1) performance of the new item could be carefully measured; (2) enough money is involved to justify funding rather expensive research procedures; (3) business managers would be willing to spend money on complex and untried market research procedures; (4) new products normally have a high failure rate; yet (5) rewards for successful introduction are often very substantial, justifying considerable consumer research expenditures. This formed the setting for what resulted in probably the most commercially successful application of multivariate market structure analysis to date.

THE MARKET STRUCTURE STUDY PROCESS

The process developed by Stefflre consists of a series of steps or blocks, interrelated, each building on the previous block or blocks. Together, they constitute a sequence of searching for new product ideas, positioning these new ideas relative to existing products/services, *evaluating* the new ideas, testing them as *concepts,* testing them in some *physical form,* and finally continuous recycling through a series of modifications until some completely satisfactory product/service form is reached. The entire process contains several

91

ingenious features; no single one of these is necessarily completely different from all previous research techniques (although some probably are), but together they constitute a complete and integrated approach to new product planning and positioning.

A *market structure study* consists of the following steps:

Phase I

1. Select market goal

2. Obtain lists of products and uses from consumers

3. Establish item-by-use matrix market definition

4. Have similarities of selected new product concepts judged

5. Conduct small-scale test of preferences for new product concepts

6. Conduct large-scale test of new product concepts

7. Select the most promising new product concept

Phase II

8. Select appropriate words, colors, textures, pictures, shapes, and so on, for the new product concept

9. Conduct a series of recyclings, including modifications and consumer testing of the proposed product

10. Test market the final new product form

Each of these steps is described in detail below.

PHASE I: SELECTING THE PRODUCT CONCEPT

Selection of Market Goal

The aim of this portion of the research is to define the market within which the new product will compete, determine the patterns of substitution and competition that exist between the current products, and determine the features that "position" current products where they fit in this structure and facilitate the development of new product descriptions and test (1) how many people prefer each description to all of the currently available products, (2) which old products each of the new-product descriptions takes its choice from, and (3) which types of people prefer which products and what descriptions. [1, p.38]

The first step is to define clearly the market that management wishes to operate within—whether the object is to develop some new brand or even a specialized form of some existing product (such as coffee), or to develop some entirely new product class (such as an instant breakfast). This forces management to delimit some array of *relevant competing products,* which defines the arena within which planning efforts will be undertaken. According to Stefflre, "In general it is fair to say that the relevant competitive array may cross-cut named product classes, and is probably broader than the manufacturer expects." [1, p.39]

Obtaining Lists of Products and Uses from Consumers

After the competitive arena has been clearly defined, 20 to 30 consumers scattered throughout the country are asked for three lists: (1) of products currently in that arena, (2) of various uses to which these products are put, and (3) of other products that could be used for the same purpose(s). From this information, lists are compiled of perhaps 50 products and 50 uses which represent the major *products* that comprise the bulk of the product class of interest (plus a few peripheral products) as well as the major *uses* to which these products are put (plus a few "idiosyncratic" uses to aid in interpretation).

Item-by-Use Matrix

The approximately 50 products and 50 uses are then arrayed in matrix form, with uses displayed as columns and products as rows. An abbreviated example from the snack food study is shown in Figure 7.1 for a *single respondent.* Entries in the matrix are: 1, if the particular product is seen as "suitable" for a particular use; 0, if the product is not suitable. Approximately 30 respondents scattered throughout the country are asked to complete an item-by-use matrix. The computer then calculates, for each respondent: (1) the perceived

Figure 7.1

ITEM-USE MATRIX FOR SNACK FOODS

	01. Watching TV	02. While Drinking Beer	03. For A Low-Calorie Lunch	04. To Nibble On	05. Just By Itself	06. Almost Anytime of Day	07. With A Coke	08. For Dessert	09. Mostly In The Afternoon	10. For Kids	11. To Go Along With A Drink	12. In The Morning	13. As An Appetizer	14. For A Quick Lunch	15. With Soup	16. For Women	17. When I'm In A Rush	18. For Breakfast	19. As A Snack	20. With Coffee	21. For Very Special Occasions	22. Late At Night	23. On Warm Days	24. In The Evening	25. Three or Four Times A Day	26. Little Get-togethers	27. With Dips	28. Without Tea	29. In Between Meals	30. When I'm Working	31. To Go With A Sandwich	32. With Pie	33. Anytime I'm Thirsty	34. After School	35. When I'm Out	36. When I'm Babysitting	37. At Parties	38. When I Go Camping	39. For Adults	40. With Cheese	41. When I Want Something Swee	42. To Kill My Appetite	43. Coffee Break	44. At A Bar	45. With Cocktails	46. After A Party	47. When I'm Shopping	48. When I'm Visiting Someone	49. When I'm Nervous	50. In Cool Weather	51. With Milk	52. "Raiding The Refrigerator"	53. With Tea	54. For Men
Potato Chips 01.	1	1		1		1	1			1	1					1			1		1	1	1	1		1	1	1	1	1	1			1	1	1	1	1	1				1	1		1	1		1				1
Pretzels 02.	1	1		1	1	1	1			1	1					1			1			1	1	1		1		1	1	1				1		1	1		1					1	1			1		1				1
Nuts 03.	1	1		1	1	1	1			1	1					1			1		1	1	1	1		1		1	1	1				1		1	1	1	1					1	1			1		1				1
Cookies 04.	1			1	1	1	1	1		1		1				1			1	1		1	1	1	1	1		1	1	1	1			1	1	1		1	1		1		1				1	1	1	1	1		1	1
A Bowl of Soup 05.			1		1					1				1		1	1				1		1	1				1		1	1				1				1	1							1			1	1		1	1
Sandwich 06.	1	1		1	1	1	1			1	1			1	1	1	1		1	1		1	1	1		1			1	1				1	1	1		1	1	1							1	1		1	1	1	1	1
Cottage Cheese 07.			1											1		1	1					1	1	1				1	1	1					1	1		1	1			1						1		1	1		1	1
Canned Fruit 08.			1					1		1			1	1		1	1	1			1		1	1				1	1	1	1								1		1									1		1	1	1
Caramel Corn 09.	1	1		1	1		1		1	1	1					1			1			1	1	1				1	1				1		1		1												1			1	1
Jello 10.	1		1		1	1		1		1				1		1	1				1	1	1	1				1	1	1	1			1	1	1	1		1		1	1					1			1		1	1	1
Coca Cola 11.	1			1	1	1	1			1						1			1		1	1	1	1	1	1	1	1	1	1	1		1	1	1	1	1	1	1	1			1	1			1	1	1	1				1
Hard-Boiled Eggs 12.			1		1					1		1		1		1	1	1		1		1	1				1		1										1				1					1		1	1	1	1	1	1
Presweetened Breakfast Cereal 13.										1		1				1	1	1		1			1	1				1																				1	1	1		1
Toastems 14.										1		1				1	1	1		1			1					1																						1	1			1
Bugles 15.	1	1		1	1	1	1		1	1	1					1			1			1	1	1		1		1	1	1				1		1	1	1	1										1		1			1	1
Cheese 16.	1	1		1	1	1	1			1	1		1		1	1	1		1		1	1	1	1	1	1		1	1	1	1	1		1	1	1		1	1	1		1			1		1	1	1	1	1	1	1	1
Ice Cream 17.	1			1	1	1	1	1		1						1			1			1	1	1	1	1		1	1	1	1	1		1	1	1	1				1						1	1		1		1		1
A Piece of Cake 18.	1			1	1	1		1		1					1	1			1	1	1	1	1	1	1	1			1	1	1			1	1	1		1	1	1		1		1			1	1	1	1	1	1	1	1
Fiddle-Faddle (Like Cracker Jacks) 19.	1	1		1	1		1			1	1					1			1			1	1	1				1	1	1				1		1	1		1														1	1
Fritos 20.	1	1		1	1	1	1		1	1	1		1			1			1			1	1	1		1	1	1	1	1	1			1	1	1		1	1	1				1	1		1	1	1	1				1
Popcorn 21.	1	1		1	1		1		1	1	1					1			1			1	1	1				1	1				1	1	1	1		1										1	1				1
French Fries 22.	1	1		1	1		1			1	1					1			1			1	1	1					1	1	1				1	1	1	1	1	1							1	1	1	1			1	1
Hot Dogs 23.	1	1		1	1	1	1			1	1			1		1	1		1			1	1	1		1				1					1	1	1	1	1	1							1	1	1	1	1		1	1
A Pickle 24.	1			1	1	1				1	1					1	1		1			1	1	1		1			1	1	1			1	1	1		1	1	1								1	1	1		1		1
Milk 25.	1		1	1	1	1				1		1		1	1	1	1	1	1			1	1	1	1			1	1	1	1	1	1	1	1	1		1	1	1		1						1	1	1		1		1
Candy Bars 26.	1			1	1	1	1			1						1			1			1	1	1				1	1	1	1			1	1	1	1	1	1	1	1		1					1	1			1		1
Peanuts 27.	1	1		1	1	1	1		1	1	1					1			1			1	1	1		1		1	1	1				1	1	1	1	1	1	1				1	1		1	1	1	1		1		1
Potato Chips and Sour Cream 28.	1	1		1			1		1	1	1					1			1			1	1	1		1	1	1	1	1	1				1	1	1	1	1	1								1	1	1		1	1	1
Cold Cuts—Salami, Bologna 29.	1	1		1	1	1	1			1	1			1	1	1	1		1			1	1	1		1	1		1	1					1	1	1	1	1	1								1	1	1		1	1	1
A Hamburger Sandwich 30.	1	1		1	1	1	1			1	1			1	1	1	1		1	1		1	1	1		1				1					1	1	1	1	1	1	1						1	1	1	1		1	1	1
Pastries 31.	1			1	1	1		1		1					1	1			1	1	1	1	1	1	1	1			1	1	1			1	1	1	1	1	1	1								1	1	1	1	1	1	1
Leftovers 32.							1		1	1				1		1	1			1		1	1	1						1				1					1									1		1	1	1	1	1	1
Meat-Flavored Snacks 33.	1	1		1	1	1	1		1	1			1	1		1	1		1	1	1	1	1	1		1		1	1					1	1	1	1		1							1	1			1	1	1	1	1	1	1
Sardines 34.			1							1				1		1	1						1							1								1				1										1	1	1	1	1	1	1
Raisins 35.			1	1	1	1				1		1				1		1	1			1	1	1	1			1	1	1				1					1			1						1	1			1	1	1
Spaghetti-O's 36.										1				1		1	1			1			1	1															1										1	1	1			1	1
Beef Jerky 37.										1						1							1	1					1										1											1	1				1
Herring 38.															1								1	1						1									1												1	1			1	1
Daisys 39.															1					1		1	1		1													1												1	1				
Pizza 40.	1	1		1	1	1	1		1	1	1					1			1			1	1	1		1				1					1	1	1		1	1							1	1	1	1	1	1	1	1
Peanut Butter and Jelly Sandwich 41.	1			1	1	1				1				1		1	1		1	1		1	1	1				1	1	1				1		1			1		1							1	1	1	1	1	1
Hard Candy 42.	1			1	1	1		1		1						1			1			1	1	1				1	1	1				1	1	1		1	1		1								1	1				1
Apples 43.	1		1	1	1	1		1		1						1	1		1			1	1	1	1			1	1	1	1			1		1		1	1			1	1				1	1	1	1		1		1
Instant Breakfast 44.			1		1										1	1	1		1			1					1		1								1	1										1	1	1	1			
Cherry Pie 45.	1			1	1	1		1		1						1			1	1	1	1	1	1		1			1	1	1			1	1	1	1		1		1		1				1	1	1	1	1	1	1	1
Rolls 46.										1						1				1	1		1	1						1					1		1	1		1							1	1	1	1	1	1	1	1
Fresh Fruit 47.	1		1	1	1	1		1		1			1	1	1	1	1	1	1	1	1	1	1	1	1	1			1	1	1	1			1	1	1	1	1	1	1	1	1	1	1				1	1	1	1	1	1	1	1
Beer 48.	1	1		1	1	1			1						1			1			1	1	1		1	1	1	1		1		1		1		1	1	1	1							1	1	1	1				1
Donuts 49.				1	1					1		1				1		1		1			1					1	1	1					1				1						1					1	1	1	1			1
Shoe String Potatoes 50.	1	1		1	1	1	1			1	1					1			1			1	1	1				1	1	1	1			1		1		1	1										1	1	1	1	1	1
Cheese and Crackers 51.	1	1	1	1	1	1		1	1	1	1	1	1	1	1	1		1		1	1	1	1		1	1		1	1				1			1	1	1	1					1	1			1	1	1	1	1	1	1
A Meaty Snack 52.	1	1		1	1	1	1		1	1	1		1	1		1	1		1		1	1	1	1		1			1	1					1	1	1		1	1				1	1			1	1	1	1	1	1	1
Sausage Sticks 53.	1	1		1	1	1	1		1	1	1		1	1		1	1		1	1	1	1	1	1		1			1	1	1			1	1	1	1		1	1				1	1			1	1	1	1	1	1	1
Nabisco Snacks—Chipsters, Shapes 54.	1	1		1	1	1	1		1	1	1					1			1		1	1	1		1		1	1					1		1		1	1										1	1	1	1	1	1	1
Cheese-Flavored Popcorn 55.	1	1		1	1	1	1		1	1	1					1			1			1	1	1				1	1				1		1			1									1	1	1			1	1
Other 56.	1	1	1	1	1	1	1	1	1	1	1	1	1	1	1	1	1	1	1	1	1	1	1	1		1	1		1	1			1		1	1	1		1	1	1	1	1	1	1	1	1		1	1	1	1	1	1

similarity of each product to every other product in terms of uses,[1] and (2) the perceived similarity of each use to every other use in terms of products. This produces, in effect, a complete "intercorrelation matrix" for products and one for uses. Each matrix is then rearranged to put similar products adjacent to one another and similar uses adjacent to one another. The original input matrix is then presented in this *rearranged form,* as shown in Figure 7.2.

Inspection of this figure reveals several aspects of the structure of the market for snack foods. For example, the upper left-hand corner

---

[1]Using the similarity measure: $A2_{ij} = \dfrac{\frac{1}{2}(a_{xi} + a_{xj} - | a_{xi} - a_{xj}|)}{\frac{1}{2}(\text{Tot col } i + \text{Tot col } j)}$

Figure 7.2

REARRANGED ITEM-USE MATRIX FOR SNACK FOODS

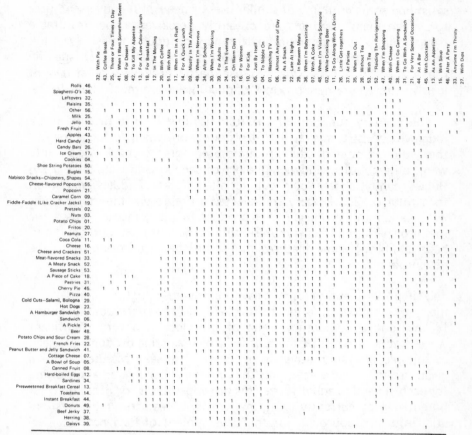

shows that this respondent perceived a group of similar foods (raisins, milk, jello, fresh fruit, apples) to be suitable for satisfying a group of similar uses (after school, when I'm working, for men, in cool weather, for adults, in the evening, on warm days, etc.). Note the rather wide range of uses that are considered "similar" in terms of products that are suitable for satisfying them. This provides an entirely different perspective on the way in which people perceive products (as meeting *needs,* rather than in terms of product characteristics or verbal stereotypes).

Inspection of item-use matrices for each respondent and for all respondents combined provides such information as: (1) products that are considered most similar across all uses; (2) uses considered most similar across all products; (3) which products are seen as appropriate for what uses; (4) which uses are seen as appropriate for what products; (5) "gaps" in the market where hardly any products are seen as satisfying some grouping of similar uses or needs; (6) conversely, uses for which many products are presently perceived as being suitable (suggesting lesser opportunities for new product entries); (7) rank ordering of products considered most appropriate for *each* specific use; and so on. Clearly, the item-use matrix provides a great deal of insight into where new product opportunities are most likely to lie.

The primary function of the item-use matrix is to provide (on a judgment basis) a smaller list of products on which to focus for further study. Some of the products used for the snack food study were: a hamburger sandwich, a piece of cake, a sandwich, beef jerky, Bugles, candy, cheese, cold cuts, cookies, Fiddle Faddles, and so on to a total of 25. These were selected to represent the major items with which the proposed new product might compete, plus some minor or peripheral items representing corners of the market and perhaps exhibiting some features that might be incorporated into the new product.

The present authors feel that the item-use matrix represents a major original contribution to the field of market structure analysis. It lays out a competing arena of products in a very significant way—that is, in terms of the *uses* for which existing products are seen as suitable, the alternative products that are seen as suitable for a given use (and vice versa), and the *semantics* considered appropriate for each general product type. This provides a basis for deciding what potential gaps currently exist, and it should lead to a more systematic, informed approach for the development of new product descriptions.

Judged Similarities

For this step, the list of 25 snacks is presented to 50 consumers scattered throughout the country; each subject is asked, for each snack product, what other products on the list he or she judges to be most similar. Subjects are also asked *in what ways* things they judge as similar are similar.

Similarities among products are expressed in terms of the proportion of the sample who say they feel the products are similar. These proportions constitute a complete matrix of "intercorrelations" among all 25 products. These similarities measures are entered into any one of several computer programs (e.g., conventional factor analysis) that identify basic groupings of similar items, and these groupings form the axes or dimensions of a perceptual positioning map—either two- or three-dimensional. Each product is "scored" on each dimension and plotted in the usual manner.

Inspection of the resulting configuration reveals more clearly what each axis or dimension might represent (this is inferred from the factor loadings or scores of the various products on the axis) and shows the "market structure" of the 25 existing products in the arena of interest. This particular analytic step is quite comparable to that of multidimensional scaling (Chapter 3), wherein *objects are compared directly as to how similar they are judged to be on an overall basis,* using a metric scale (rather than rankings) for measurement purposes.

Referring to this stage, Stefflre states:

> Now it is somewhere around the edges or interstices of this structure that we are going to put our new product. We do not know, at this point, whether there are large amounts of consumer demand unmet by the current products, but we do have a model that gives us a rough idea as to the structure interrelating the currently available products. We also have a list of all of the things said about each of the products to help us guess what features of each product lead it to be placed as it is in this structure. [1, p. 43]

This positioning map is used to generate 25 to 30 new product descriptions, which include: (1) descriptions of potential products incorporating features of some of the products currently in the class; (2) descriptions representing products considered particularly important to understand; (3) descriptions representing new combinations of features currently in the product class; (4) descriptions bringing in *new* features found in products *near* the class; and (5) descriptions bringing in words not used currently in describing this type of product but implied as suitable for this area by Sperber's Law.[2]

Such descriptions as the following were generated from the perceptual map of existing snack foods: a snack the whole family en-

---

[2]Sperber's Law suggests that when one word in a semantic field takes on a new meaning, other words in the same field will follow along into this new domain.

joys, an energy snack, a snack you can drink, a nibbly snack, a nibbly fish snack, a toaster pizza, a candy made from whole fruit, a snack for the lunch box, and so on. These descriptions are a product of art rather than science, of course; they represent "informed guesses" as to new products that *might* be of interest to the public. Even so, at least there is some basis of measurement and fact to guide creative thinking into areas that are potentially more fruitful.

Small-Scale Test of Product Concepts

The next step is to "test" the 25 to 30 new product descriptions in some preliminary way. This is usually done by asking a sample of 200 subjects nationwide to rank (in terms of preference) the 25 to 30 descriptions *mixed in with* the 25 existing products that were used to construct the earlier positioning map. Subjects are also asked to rank the product they currently use most frequently and their "favorite" product. These rankings provide the data for several rather crucial analyses:

1. What proportion of the sample *prefers* each of the new product descriptions to:
   —All 25 familiar products
   —The product each respondent uses most frequently
   —Each respondent's favorite product
   —Any part of the above

2. Which items (either existing products or descriptions) are liked by the same individuals

These data are first used to compare directly the preference for each new description to both the respondent's favorite product and the most frequently used products. Those products scoring high across all respondents are obviously prime candidates for continued consideration.

Another positioning map is then constructed which includes both the 25 to 30 new product descriptions and the 25 existing products. In contrast to the previous map, which was based on *perceptions of similarities* among existing products, the second map is based on the *preference rankings* assigned to *both* new and existing products by the 200 respondents.

Technically, the map is developed by intercorrelating the preference ranks of each product and description to establish a complete correlation matrix for all items. This matrix is processed by conventional factor analysis (or any similar dimensionalizing procedure) to extract the most important two or three dimensions, which then serve as axes of the map. Note that these are preference, not similarities, vectors, so the resulting configuration represents a preference mapping of the product arena with the new product descriptions included. Each vector represents some preference construct that is different from the others. Various new product description terms serve as identification benchmarks to assist in determining the meaning of each vector, and selected demographics (e.g., age, sex) are interspersed to suggest the types of people for which each product or description would be most suitable.

From all of this (direct comparisons of preference rankings plus the preference map), five preferred new descriptions are selected for the next step. One additional relatively unattractive description ("a dog") is also selected to aid in interpretation.

Large-Scale Test of Concepts

These six new product descriptions are then "tested" in telephone interviews with a national sample of 1,500 subjects. The six descriptions, plus the respondent's favorite product *and* his or her most frequently used product, are presented in sets of four to be ranked in order of preference. Since these sets of four contain comparisons between all possible pairs of objects, an intraindividual rank ordering of all items can be computed. The data can also be used to compute what would be likely to happen in a variety of choice situations, since each item has been paired with every other.

In a study of the dessert market, Stefflre was able to see *how many respondents preferred each new product description to the desserts they ate most frequently.* He could also identify *which of the existing dessert products each new description took its choices from.* In addition, Stefflre's data showed what types of people (e.g., age, sex) liked each new description. The bulk of this information is summarized in Table 7.1.

Note, for example, that the description "a rich dessert" takes 5 of 231 choices received by Jello, for a 2.2 percent "draw" from this dessert. This means that of the 231 respondents who said Jello was

Table 7.1

DRAW RATIOS OF DESCRIPTIONS FROM BRANDS

Product	Arch Dessert	A Cooling Refreshing Ready-To-Eat Dessert	A Fresh, Nibbly Fruit Dessert	A Healthy Dessert	A Light But Satisfying Dessert	A Crisp, Fancy Dessert
Jello	$\frac{5}{5+226}=0.0216$	$\frac{30}{30+201}=0.1299$	$\frac{14}{14+217}=0.0606$	$\frac{26}{26+205}=0.1126$	$\frac{23}{23+208}=0.0996$	$\frac{9}{9+222}=0.0390$
Gelatin	$\frac{0}{0+1}=0.$	$\frac{0}{0+1}=0.$	$\frac{0}{0+1}=0.$	$\frac{0}{0+1}=0.$	$\frac{0}{0+1}=0.$	$\frac{0}{0+1}=0.$
Whip N' Chill	$\frac{1}{1+5}=0.1667$	$\frac{1}{1+5}=0.1667$	$\frac{1}{1+5}=0.1667$	$\frac{0}{0+6}=0.$	$\frac{1}{1+5}=0.1667$	$\frac{0}{0+6}=0.$
Pudding	$\frac{2}{2+42}=0.0455$	$\frac{4}{4+40}=0.0909$	$\frac{3}{3+41}=0.0682$	$\frac{6}{6+30}=0.1364$	$\frac{7}{7+37}=0.1591$	$\frac{6}{6+38}=0.1364$
Chocolate Pudding	$\frac{0}{0+10}=0.$	$\frac{1}{1+9}=0.1000$	$\frac{0}{0+10}=0.$	$\frac{0}{0+10}=0.$	$\frac{2}{2+6}=0.2000$	$\frac{1}{1+9}=0.1000$
Rice Pudding	$\frac{0}{0+4}=0.$	$\frac{0}{0+4}=0.$	$\frac{1}{1+3}=0.2500$	$\frac{0}{0+4}=0.$	$\frac{0}{0+4}=0.$	$\frac{0}{0+4}=0.$
Custard	$\frac{0}{0+5}=0.$	$\frac{1}{1+4}=0.2000$	$\frac{0}{0+5}=0.$	$\frac{1}{1+4}=0.2000$	$\frac{1}{1+4}=0.2000$	$\frac{1}{1+4}=0.2000$
Junket	$\frac{1}{1+1}=0.5000$	$\frac{0}{0+2}=0.$	$\frac{0}{0+2}=0.$	$\frac{1}{1+1}=0.5000$	$\frac{0}{0+2}=0.$	$\frac{1}{1+1}=0.5000$
Tapioca	$\frac{0}{0+4}=0.$	$\frac{2}{2+2}=0.5000$	$\frac{0}{0+4}=0.$	$\frac{1}{1+3}=0.2500$	$\frac{0}{0+4}=0.$	$\frac{0}{0+4}=0.$
Pastry	$\frac{1}{1+11}=0.0833$	$\frac{2}{2+10}=0.1667$	$\frac{1}{1+11}=0.0833$	$\frac{1}{1+11}=0.0833$	$\frac{0}{0+12}=0.$	$\frac{1}{1+11}=0.0833$
Pie	$\frac{17}{17+238}=0.0667$	$\frac{33}{33+222}=0.1294$	$\frac{18}{18+237}=0.0706$	$\frac{29}{29+226}=0.1137$	$\frac{33}{33+222}=0.1294$	$\frac{22}{22+233}=0.0863$
Cheese	$\frac{0}{0+0}=0.$	$\frac{0}{0+0}=0.$	$\frac{0}{0+0}=0.$	$\frac{0}{0+0}=0.$	$\frac{0}{0+0}=0.$	$\frac{0}{0+0}=0.$
Fruit	$\frac{5}{5+93}=0.0510$	$\frac{11}{11+87}=0.1122$	$\frac{10}{10+88}=0.1020$	$\frac{6}{6+92}=0.0612$	$\frac{17}{17+81}=0.1735$	$\frac{6}{6+92}=0.0812$
Fruit Cocktail	$\frac{0}{0+11}=0.$	$\frac{1}{1+10}=0.0909$	$\frac{0}{0+11}=0.$	$\frac{2}{2+9}=0.1818$	$\frac{0}{0+11}=0.$	$\frac{0}{0+11}=0.$
Fresh Fruit	$\frac{0}{0+41}=0.$	$\frac{6}{6+35}=0.1463$	$\frac{2}{2+39}=0.0488$	$\frac{4}{4+37}=0.0976$	$\frac{3}{3+38}=0.0732$	$\frac{1}{1+40}=0.0244$
Cooked Fruit	$\frac{0}{0+17}=0.$	$\frac{2}{2+15}=0.1176$	$\frac{0}{0+17}=0.$	$\frac{1}{1+16}=0.0588$	$\frac{2}{2+15}=0.1176$	$\frac{0}{0+17}=0.$
Specific Fruit	$\frac{1}{1+31}=0.0313$	$\frac{2}{2+30}=0.0625$	$\frac{2}{2+30}=0.0625$	$\frac{2}{2+30}=0.0625$	$\frac{2}{2+30}=0.0625$	$\frac{1}{1+31}=0.0313$
Apple Sauce	$\frac{0}{0+4}=0.$	$\frac{1}{1+3}=0.2500$	$\frac{0}{0+4}=0.$	$\frac{1}{1+3}=0.2500$	$\frac{2}{2+2}=0.5000$	$\frac{0}{0+4}=0.$
Strawberry Shortcake	$\frac{0}{0+17}=0.$	$\frac{2}{2+15}=0.1176$	$\frac{2}{2+15}=0.1176$	$\frac{2}{2+15}=0.1176$	$\frac{0}{0+17}=0.$	$\frac{2}{2+15}=0.1176$
Cake	$\frac{11}{11+209}=0.0500$	$\frac{36}{36+184}=0.1636$	$\frac{18}{18+202}=0.0818$	$\frac{20}{20+200}=0.0909$	$\frac{28}{28+192}=0.1273$	$\frac{23}{23+197}=0.1045$
Other	$\frac{0}{0+10}=0.$	$\frac{0}{0+10}=0.$	$\frac{2}{2+8}=0.2000$	$\frac{3}{3+7}=0.3000$	$\frac{1}{1+9}=0.1000$	$\frac{0}{0+10}=0.$
Ice Cream	$\frac{10}{10+346}=0.0281$	$\frac{52}{52+304}=0.1461$	$\frac{17}{17+339}=0.0478$	$\frac{38}{38+318}=0.1067$	$\frac{42}{42+314}=0.1180$	$\frac{25}{25+331}=0.0702$
Ice Cream A La Mode	$\frac{2}{2+3}=0.4000$	$\frac{4}{4+1}=0.8000$	$\frac{0}{0+5}=0.$	$\frac{2}{2+3}=0.4000$	$\frac{1}{1+4}=0.2000$	$\frac{1}{1+4}=0.2000$
Ice Cream & Cookies	$\frac{0}{0+9}=0.$	$\frac{0}{0+0}=0.$	$\frac{0}{0+0}=0.$	$\frac{0}{0+0}=0.$	$\frac{0}{0+0}=0.$	$\frac{0}{0+0}=0.$
Cookies	$\frac{2}{2+22}=0.0833$	$\frac{2}{2+22}=0.0833$	$\frac{2}{2+22}=0.0833$	$\frac{1}{1+23}=0.0417$	$\frac{3}{3+21}=0.1250$	$\frac{2}{2+22}=0.0833$
Other Products	$\frac{0}{0+12}=0.$	$\frac{4}{4+8}=0.3333$	$\frac{0}{0+12}=0.$	$\frac{0}{0+12}=0.$	$\frac{0}{0+12}=0.$	$\frac{0}{0+12}=0.$

their favorite dessert, only 5 said they would prefer "a rich dessert" to Jello. This compares with the 17 people who would prefer this description to pie, a 6.7 percent draw.

Another way to look at the same data is to calculate the contribution of each familar dessert to the total number of choices received by each description. For example, Jello contributes 5 choices, or 8.6 percent, of the total of 58 choices received by "a rich dessert"—as compared to 17 choices, or 29.3 percent, contributed by pie.

One can also note the total number of choices all new descriptions *combined* were able to take from the group of established products: if this number is especially low (or high) it probably suggests a particularly bad (or good) assortment of new product descriptions in toto. This would be rather crucial information in helping the manufacturer decide how vulnerable a certain product class, as a whole, is to penetration by *any* new product.

The draw ratio analysis might be considered another major contribution of Stefflre to the new product search process. While firms often compare new product ideas against existing products, they do not usually test so many ideas in so systematic a fashion as the draw ratio analysis provides.

Selection of Most Promising Concept

These shares of choices, or draws, are considered projectable to the national market, and they constitute the criterion used to select a new product description that will meet the market share goals set by the manufacturer. The final description(s) selected for further refinement is "evolved" from a study of Table 7.1 plus all other previous relevant information.

Stefflre states:

The problem in new product development is not so much, in our opinion, "having the big idea." There are a large number of simple ideas, a consistent execution of which will tap a tremendous volume of unmet consumer demand. A good idea is necessary but not sufficient in building new products. [1, p. 59]

PHASE II:

REFINING THE FINAL PRODUCT CONCEPT

After the final product concept has been selected, Phase II (steps 8, 9, and 10) begins. This phase consists of a series of six rounds which modify and retest: (1) the product concept itself, (2) the packaging, (3) the advertising themes, and (4) the product name. These components must be developed to the point where they perform as well as the original target specifications. The phase is called "component generation and evaluation." The early rounds focus on what attributes (taste, smell, color, texture, feel, shape, form, etc.) "fit" the target description plus selected minor modifications of this description.

In this regard, Stefflre states:

The problem of analysis of a complex multiattribute set of natural objects into components and then synthesis of new items through recombination of these components into new combinations embodied in new complex multiattribute objects and/or events which have predictable meanings to members of a culture, is much the type of problem found in speech analysis and synthesis or in the learning and use of a natural language. The attempt to take a new product description and its words and/or phrases and embody these in a physical representation . . . that will match the verbal description and perform like it in terms of matching consumer demand and eliciting patterns of belief and behavior, can be seen as a problem in translation— from words to objects and events with the meaning held constant if a translation is made back into words (back translation). [1, p. 61]

The basic procedures developed to effect this matching of product description with specific product attributes are of three major types: X-est, scales, and balanced madness. Each of these is designed to help translate the new product *description* into the colors, shapes, textures, symbols, and illustrations (pictures) that can be used to build the new product *form* that matches the description. This new product form is then tested with large samples to see that it in fact performs like the description it was built to match, prior to market introduction.

102

X-est

The first step, X-est, consists of asking a sample of respondents to select from a very large array the "items" (colors, shapes, sizes, textures, etc.) that best fit some description, word, or phrase. The latter refers to the semantics of the new product—the short description selected for the product plus other words of phrases that might be used to describe it on the package or in an advertisement. Thus, if the new product is to be a "happy pickle," the respondent selects the happi*est* (X-est) color, shape, size, texture, or whatever.

For example, respondents are presented with "color wheels" containing squares of hundreds of different hues, arranged sequentially through the color spectrum. They are asked to select those colors that best fit the new product description (or word, or phrase.) They are also shown color combination wheels that allow them to form their own *pairs of colors* that best fit the description.

Analysis consists of tabulating the frequency with which each of the colors (and pairs of colors) is selected as matching each of the 10 to 25 descriptions, words, or phrases. Also, a calculation is made of the ratio of this observed frequency to the frequency expected based on (1) the number of times the particular *description* (or word or phrase) is matched to any color, and (2) the number of times the color is matched to any description. Both observed and observed/expected frequencies provide a crude measure of which colors best fit the final product description (or some other description, word, or phrase) being tested. The final color combination is evolved using this analysis (plus tests of a limited number of viable alternative color combinations.).

This same general procedure is used also for selecting possible forms or shapes for the container, textures for the product itself and the container, symbols for labels or for an appropriate trademark, and pictures for the labels and advertisements. The search for each of these items starts with a large number of specific items within the category (e.g., colors, pictures) that are narrowed down sequentially to some final set that does not present too onerous a burden for respondents.

Figure 7.3 illustrates the final output from this process by showing the various pictures, shades, and shapes or forms that respondents most closely associated with the single word "clean." Specifics of

103

Figure 7.3

PHYSICAL CHARACTERISTICS ASSOCIATED
WITH THE WORD "CLEAN"

this type give much clearer direction for decisions involving the product itself, the container, the product name, and creative promotional efforts. During these early rounds, Stefflre maintains,

> one is buying information about the meaning of stimuli to consumers and the demand among consumers for a variety of types of materials. Heterogeneous materials manufactured or obtained cheaply and in great variety should be tested early to give direction to the creation of the legally, economically, and practically possible alternatives to be tested later and finally introduced into the market. [1, p. 81]

Scales

For this analysis, consumers rate groups of two to fifteen items (colors, pictures, etc.) on a scale as to: (1) *how well* they fit a selected product description (or word or phrase), and (2) their *preference* for each of the items presented. The resulting data are analyzed in two ways:

1. Tabulation of observed ratings and use of averages to determine how well the item fits the product concept.

2. Determination of proportion of people who prefer each *new* item evaluated (name, description, copy theme, ad, product, package, etc.) to the array of existing competing products

The results provide additional insight into which colors, shapes, and the like best suit one or more of the final new product descriptions.

Balanced Madness

This third step is similar to the scales analysis. It consists of asking respondents to rank 50 items; included in the list are a mixture of names of the respondent's own favorite or frequently used products, ten to fifteen names or ads of *current* products, fifteen new product *descriptions* (representing several alternative approaches or types of product formulations that differ in meaningful ways), five new product *names,* and ten or so *ads* for the new products. Several analyses can be made from these rankings:

1. The researcher can determine the proportion of consumers (or of consumers' purchasing volume) preferring each new product

or name or ad description to the existing competitive array of products, names, and ads.

2. Analyses can be made of the fit of each of the ten or so ads to the target description (if the product itself has not stabilized) or to the new product itself (if it has stabilized), based on the *correlations* of the rankings of the ads with either the target concept or with other serious product idea candidates.

3. Correlations can also be made between rankings of the new product descriptions, rankings of new product *samples* (on a blind testing basis), various new product names, and selected descriptive statements (e.g., friendly, bright, bitter).

4. The correlations in no. 3 can be analyzed using a technique like factor analysis to produce a "final" preference positioning map, showing the spatial positionings of the blind products/ads/names near the descriptions they match best.

Thus, the market structure study process starts with simple and crude products or ads and moves in an evolutionary fashion toward ever more polished and refined products/ads with a level of finish on a par with those currently in the marketplace.

ADVANTAGES AND LIMITATIONS

Advantages

Stefflre's process almost certainly constitutes the most comprehensive *systems approach* to new product concept development to date. Initially the system is linear, with each step building on the one immediately preceding it and in turn providing the foundation for the next step. When a single "target description" has been selected, the system becomes circular (Phase II) in the sense of exploring, evaluating, and refining the product description through a series of recyclings, at which time it investigates the most appropriate components (colors, textures, packaging, pictures, advertisements, etc.) for the target description. This sequence does not limit the investigator to the original product concept; rather, it enables him to compare that idea with others that may appear as the work progresses and to shift the emphasis to those newer ideas that seem to have even greater potential. There are, of course, the usual organizational problems that occur when a project "shifts gears" to focus on other ideas that emerge as the work progresses.

Positioning maps (of both similarities and preferences) are constructed at several stages within the total process to provide visual displays for better understanding and communication. They are particularly valuable in the rather frequent meetings with management and with venture teams formed within the company to execute the development and introduction of the new product.

The item-use matrix, in particular, may be the single most important contribution Stefflre makes to the new product/service search process. It provides a structured conceptual framework for understanding the relationship between currently available products and the *uses* or needs perceived as suitable for each product, and vice versa. Computer analysis extends this notion to find *groupings* of similar products suitable for groupings of similar uses, to develop a more comprehensive and orderly "structure" for a given market.

Stefflre's experience has shown that the draw ratio and similar analyses (scales, balanced madness are crucial to providing meaningful estimates of share of market and most likely competing products. These analyses are beyond anything normally done as part of conventional positioning studies.

Limitations

While a market structure study is a mixture of both art and science, art clearly predominates. This seems reasonable, given the "systems" approach to the product planning process envisioned by Stefflre. He makes no claim that his technology is superior to others —technology in the sense of the grouping algorithms used for rearranging the item-use matrix and for developing the various perceptual and preference positioning maps constructed in the course of a study.

Since various grouping algorithms tend to produce similar results when applied to the same body of similarities measures, it is not likely that any serious flaws can be demonstrated with these portions of a total study. The similarities measures themselves are either correlations or are based on the index developed by Stefflre especially for the item-use matrix (see footnote 1); this index seems appropriate to the nature of the data on which it is based. In summary, the technology seems very adequate for the tasks.

One wonders if all of the various steps, approaches, positioning maps, and so on are really necessary. Since every step adds expense (sometimes a considerable amount), would it be possible to skip some steps or recyclings in favor of "educated guesses" by seasoned creative marketing and/or advertising personnel? Stefflre would undoubtedly argue that with stakes as high as they are for a new product, and with probabilities of success as low as they commonly are, the extra dollars are indeed justified if they prevent mistakes of the type that are quite common given the (often conflicting) "suboptimal" objectives of the key people both within and outside the firm. Conceptually at least, a product built to the specifications of a market structure study almost "cannot fail" (a risky statement, of course, in view of the great complexities of the marketplace); certainly its chances *should* be much greater than those of a product conceived and executed in the usual manner.

More specifically, one wonders why Stefflre makes almost no effort to determine early in the process the relative sizes of the markets for alternative competing new product descriptions. How *often* does a person have a cold, use each snack food or dessert, and so on? This is left for the final recyclings, where draw ratios are computed for each variation on the final target new product descriptions. Why not obtain some estimate of potential volume when respondents construct the item-use matrix? Perhaps this extra step, plus increasing the number of subjects for this phase of the study, would result in focusing on larger markets at a much earlier stage.

While Stefflre's batting average has been quite high for products that have actually been introduced using this procedure, some product planners feel that it is an oversimplification to say that developing a new product is a "linear" process, in the sense of a step-by-step procession with each step-building on the previous one(s). Some feel that the decisions and choices made in, say, step 2 or step 3 cannot always be made satisfactorily without considering the implications in, say, step 5 or step 6. The linear process tends to engender a false sense of security which distracts from viewing all considerations (i.e., price, distribution, advertising, possible government reactions) simultaneously to ensure a good fit. In other words, one tends to lose the *Gestalt* of the proposed new product.

There is also the possibility that the whole product may be different from the sum of its parts. For example, again suppose the objective were to develop a "happy pickle." The market structure process would identify a "happy" color, shape, texture, taste, and so on. When these separate elements were combined into a single product form, however, it is *possible* that the result would not be a happy pickle because of unfavorable "interaction effects" among the various elements. The present authors do not feel that this is likely to happen often enough to warrant concern, but the reader should be aware of it. If this did occur it would be revealed in the various tests of the whole product in later testing phases.

From a managerial standpoint, there are other possible problems (which are not unique to the market structure study process, incidentally). The various "pieces" or components of the product that are evolved in the course of the study are dictated by how well they fit the product "bundle" *from the viewpoint of the consumer.* However, various representatives of the business firm (labs, product planners, product managers, top management, ad agency) often have their own ideas as to what one or more specific details of the final product should be like. This leads to conflict, which can only be resolved by someone or some committee high in the managerial ranks, and it is by no means always resolved in favor of the market structure study results.

An even more serious problem is that this type of study requires a large commitment of funds in the beginning, with no clear idea as to what the final product will be like. In contrast, the usual source of new product ideas is the company developmental labs or the ad agency. These sources do not represent any *incremental* cost for a given idea, and the idea usually shows up either in physical prototype or in working drawings or blueprints. Only companies that have experienced the vast inefficiencies or disappointments that often accompany this conventional approach have been willing to commit the large sums of money required for a market structure study.

In sum, all of these limitations are moot. Their importance depends entirely on one's perspective and objectives in new product development. Certainly a market structure study represents a substantial contribution to the technology of new product planning; at the very least it has provided new tools and conceptualizations to broaden the perspectives of both researcher and planner.

REFERENCE TO CHAPTER 7

1. Stefflre, Volney. *New Products and New Enterprises: A Report on an Experiment in Applied Social Science.* Irvine: School of Social Science, University of California, Irvine, 1971.

Chapter 8

BENEFIT STRUCTURE ANALYSIS

The perceptual and preference mapping techniques discussed in Chapters 3 through 5 provide very useful ways of structuring markets; however, they are most appropriate for product/service categories that are relatively narrowly defined, such as compact cars, toothpastes, airlines, banks, orange-juice-type drinks, service stations, breakfast cereals, and the like. Nonmetric scaling can be used for broader category definitions, but it seldom is (on a commercial basis); and, when used, it often produces two- or three-dimensional maps that seem to oversimplify and obscure the full complexities and richness of a broad category of consumer needs.

Stefflre's work expands significantly on conventional perceptual mapping models by supplying tools (e.g., the item-use matrix) for structuring much broader product categories such as nonprescription drugs and pharmaceuticals, snack foods, desserts, various types of languages, and the like. It does this in a manner that provides far more detailed insight into consumer needs than do nonmetric scaling techniques. Thus, Stefflre's work places greater emphasis on a variety of *specific benefits desired* than do any of the conventional positioning techniques.

But even the Stefflre market structure study has tended to confine itself to relatively narrow product/service categories. In addition, data in item-use matrices are analyzed and evaluated for only a few (25) respondents on essentially a clinical basis, rather than aggregating across several hundred respondents to develop a more detailed and objective "structure" for a given market. New products or services that are really different require even better developmental tools to locate unfilled gaps in very broad consumer need areas.

111

Consider, for example, the case of a company interested in developing some entirely new form of banking service (e.g., the bank credit card), or a company looking toward an entirely new type of synthetic food product (e.g., an instant breakfast), or a company interested in a new type of tool suitable for many different types of home repair or redecoration tasks, or a company looking for entirely new types of beverages. *In such cases what is required is a deeper understanding of consumer needs in terms of specific benefits and groupings of benefits desired by large numbers of consumers, to provide a wide range of satisfactions in complex need situations.* A technique called *benefit structure analysis* was developed by one of the present authors to systematically search for needs in broadly defined markets [1].

Objectives

A benefit structure study is quite broad in purpose and execution. Like the perceptual mapping studies discussed earlier, it may be used to direct product development or to provide clues for product repositioning. The study is comprehensive in that product benefits, attributes, situational variables, consumer needs, and the like, may all be included in the measurement phase and their relationships determined in the analysis phase. The study is designed with two primary objectives:

1. To identify the most important consumer needs within a broad need area and to measure the relative importance of these needs in quantitative terms

2. To measure the extent to which each of these important needs is not now being met, also in quantitative terms

Knowledge of the size of both needs and need deficiencies offers direction for product improvement or new product development.

Developing an Exhaustive Compendium of Benefits

In contrast to typical attitude measurement studies which consider 10 to 15 product features or attributes (e.g., speed, styling, handling qualities of a motorcycle), a benefit structure study will usually cover up to 100 very specific benefits. Thus, respondents interested in motorcycles might be asked to what extent they want each of such specific satisfactions as:

112

—Feeling of control over a powerful machine

—Able to go places a car won't go

—Easy maintenance

—Thrills from doing something dangerous

—Good to use for errands

—Having fun with friends

—Meeting a challenge

—Psyches me up

—Enjoy working on it

The greater the variety and imagination of such statements the better. Many of these will overlap somewhat, and the purpose of later structural analysis is to determine the extent and pattern of these overlapping relationships. It is therefore wise to start with too many specific benefits rather than too few and to let the computer do the necessary data reduction to find the more "general" benefit factors (groups of similar specific benefits) sought by motorcycle enthusiasts. Focus group interviews, as well as individual in-depth interviews, are a helpful first step to uncovering all possible types of benefits sought, including "rational" ones as well as those that respondents are less willing to admit. The important thing is to make sure that every specific benefit and every *type* of benefit is included. The final list should be reasonably exhaustive.

Sometimes the initial listing of benefits is too large to be used in later full-scale field interviewing; the number may reach 150-200. In this case, preliminary field interviews with 200 respondents can reduce the overlap and eliminate duplicate and triplicate statements, using factor analysis or other data-reduction techniques. No more than 100 specific benefits (preferably less) should be used in the final questionnaire.

To illustrate the technique of benefit structure analysis, a study of household cleaning products is presented here. This study is hypothetical, but the data shown are actual results from a composite of three separate commercial studies conducted by one of the authors in broad product areas.

BENEFIT STRUCTURE FOR HOUSEHOLD CLEANING PRODUCTS: QUALITATIVE PHASE

Household cleaning products were defined as *any product used to clean surfaces within the home other than rugs, drapes, or for dusting purposes.* Examples of products that fit this definition are Ajax, Lysol, 409, ammonia, Glo Coat, and Windex.

This study began with a series of 50 individual interviews (for most studies, focus group of 25-50 would work as well). The interviewer asked the subject to recall all occasions when she cleaned any interior surfaces *during the day prior to the interview.* For each of these occasions she was asked:

1. What was the cleaning chore? (e.g., sink, floor—(Table 8.1)

2. What benefits were sought or what were the objectives of this cleaning exercise? (Table 8.2)

3. What products were used in this operation? (type and brand)

4. What were the characteristics or attributes of the product? (Table 8.3)

Table 8.1

EXAMPLES OF OBJECTS CLEANED

Toilet bowls	Stove tops
Sinks	Diaper pails
Counters	Cabinet facings
Spots on walls	Linoleum
Spots on floors	Paneling
Bathtubs	Lamps
Shower stalls	Aluminum
Small appliances	Windows
Tile surfaces	Upholstery

Table 8.2
EXAMPLES OF BENEFITS DESIRED

Bleaches	Chrome sparkles
Removes stains	Doesn't dull
Removes grease	Makes me feel good
Removes built-up dirt	Doesn't hurt hands
Cleans tub ring	Dissolves grease
Less elbow grease	Can use as much as needed
Can see it work	Doesn't remove gloss from paint
Cleans cracks (grout) better	Boosts detergents
Doesn't leave residue	Strips wax
No rinsing necessary	Less build up
Doesn't damage surfaces	Lets color come through
Kills mildew	Stands up to damp mopping
Disinfects	Seals porous floors

5. What applicator, if any, was used? (e.g., mop, brush, sponge, rag)

6. What time of day was the work done?

Table 8.3
EXAMPLES OF
PRODUCT CHARACTERISTICS

Strong smell	Biodegradable
Abrasive/scratchy	Concentrated
Thin liquid	Self-polishing
Low suds	Sprays on
Quick drying	Attractive color
Wipes on	Contains deodorant
Dark color	Economical
Caustic	Pine smell

In this study, it was also necessary to ask about any other cleaning tasks done during the week, month, or over the year, since many items are cleaned only on a very infrequent basis by some households (windows, refrigerator, drip pans, etc.). Using these lists of products, attributes, benefits, cleaning occasions, and the like, it was then possible to design a large-scale quantitative study to determine the structural relationships of these elements.

QUANTITATIVE PHASE: METHODOLOGY

The quantitative phase of a benefit structure study is aimed at determining the degree to which each benefit is *desired* by the consumer for each usage (in this case, cleaning) occasion and the extent to which desired benefits *are or are not being received.*

In this study, a nationwide survey of 500 female heads of household was conducted in metropolitan areas. A rather lengthy in-house interview began by questioning the subject about all cleaning occasions that she encountered the previous day. Going through the entire day, she told what cleaning chores she did and what products were used for each occasion.

After this cataloging process was completed, the interviewer selected *one* cleaning occasion mentioned by the respondent, using a rotational sampling pattern. This one occasion then became the focus of a much more intensive probe about cleaning and cleaning products. *This random cross section of one cleaning occasion should represent total U.S. household cleaning occasions* (within usual survey limitations). Care must be taken in survey timing, however, since patterns may differ over different days of the week and by time of year (e.g., spring cleaning).

For this one occasion, each subject was asked the degree to which each benefit (from the list in Table 8.2) was *wanted;* then she was asked the degree to which it was *received* on that same cleaning occasion. For these measurements, a four-point scale was used: 4=a whole lot, 3=pretty much, 2=somewhat, 1=not at all.[1] Thus, for example, a respondent might report that when cleaning her linoleum floor the preceding day she wanted the benefit "cleans without scrubbing" "a whole lot" (4), but that she received it only "somewhat" (2). Therefore, she would have a benefit deficiency of 2 (4-2).

---

[1] The verbal descriptors for each scale point were selected based on a pretest using the Thurstone equal-appearing interval technique; thus, the scale should have metric (or near metric) properties.

Subjects were also asked what product and brand (if any) was used during this cleaning occasion. Then they were asked to identify product characteristics using the list of attributes developed in the qualitative phase (Table 8.3). The list of applicators was also reviewed to determine if any of these were employed for this cleaning occasion. Finally, various types of supporting information were collected, such as: (1) how often the respondent cleans this item, (2) time of day, (3) other persons present, and (4) activities both before and after the cleaning process.

The resulting data comprise a multidimensional matrix: *benefits wanted* x *benefits received* x *cleaning needs* x *products used* x *product characteristics* x *applicators* x *various supporting data*. Each dimension has from perhaps 5 to as many as 100 categories. This *n*-dimensional matrix is called the *complete benefit matrix*. It comprises the data bank for a variety of simple tabulations as well as for a wide range of multivariate analyses. Several of the more useful types of analyses are presented below.

Primary Analytic Objectives

There are so many possible ways of analyzing the complete benefit matrix that early definition of objectives is imperative. All analyses are done on an *aggregate* basis, with responses pooled across all survey respondents or across some selected subgroup of respondents. Figure 8.1 shows schematically the principal types of analyses and relationships that are usually most useful for the majority of planning purposes. Each of these is explained below, together with the many different research models and techniques required. A number of additional analyses are also valuable and would normally be an integral part of any benefit structure analysis study, but space limitations prevent their consideration here.

Product-by-Use Matrix

One of the simplest analyses initially is the product-use matrix, shown in Figure 8.2. This is similar to the Stefflre item-use matrix; it differs in that subjects are not asked which products they would "consider appropriate" for a particular cleaning use but rather which product(s) they actually used *for the particular cleaning occasion selected for the preceding day*. Since the present matrix is summed over all 500 respondents—to reveal a representative cross section of products and uses on a joint basis—it purports to represent the total

Figure 8.1

MOST USEFUL LINKAGE ANALYSES

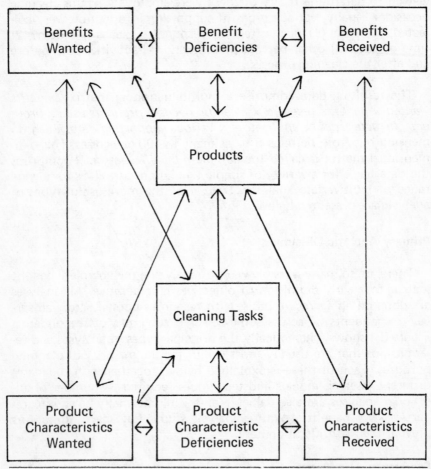

U.S. market for household cleaning products (subject to the usual limitations of consumer surveys).

This particular product-use matrix shows more concentration than is often found. For example, Product A is used almost exclusively for cleaning use no. 23, H is used for no. 5, M is used for no. 1, and so on. However, some products are clearly multi-use: C, D, F, J, and so on. Some show both dispersion and concentration, such as Products L and P. A similar analysis can easily be done for cleaning uses, to reveal patterns of product usage.

In the case of food products, such information may already be available in the "menu census"; for most broad product/use categories, however, this particular type of information is simply not available elsewhere—yet it is obtained almost as a by-product of a benefit structure analysis study.

Figure 8.2

PRODUCT–USE MATRIX

PRODUCT

	1	2	3	4	5	6	7	8	9	10	11	12	13	14	15	16	17	18	19	20	21	22	23
A	0	0	0	0	0	0	0	0	0	0	0	0	0	0	0	0	0	0	0	0	1	1	18
B	0	0	0	1	1	0	4	0	0	1	0	0	0	0	0	0	2	0	0	1	0	1	0
C	0	3	3	2	3	4	6	10	7	0	4	1	1	0	34	0	6	0	2	4	0	3	1
D	0	0	0	5	3	0	0	0	0	0	5	0	0	0	0	0	0	0	0	0	0	0	0
E	0	0	0	0	0	0	0	13	4	0	0	0	0	0	0	0	0	0	0	0	0	0	0
F	0	3	1	0	0	0	0	1	1	0	0	0	2	3	0	0	0	2	0	4	0	6	0
G	0	0	1	1	1	1	0	1	0	0	0	0	0	0	0	0	0	0	0	0	0	1	0
H	0	0	1	1	15	1	0	0	0	0	1	0	0	0	2	0	0	0	0	1	0	1	0
I	0	0	0	2	3	2	0	0	0	0	1	0	0	1	0	0	0	0	0	0	0	1	0
J	0	1	2	1	0	2	0	0	2	5	0	0	0	0	0	0	0	0	1	1	0	2	1
K	0	0	0	0	2	0	0	0	0	0	1	0	0	0	0	0	0	0	0	0	8	0	0
L	0	0	3	8	4	23	1	0	0	0	5	2	0	0	1	0	0	0	2	1	0	5	0
M	13	0	0	0	0	0	0	0	0	0	1	0	0	0	0	0	0	0	0	0	0	1	0
N	0	0	0	0	0	1	0	0	0	0	3	6	9	7	10	0	7	1	2	14	0	1	0
O	0	0	2	0	0	1	0	2	0	1	1	2	0	0	0	0	0	0	0	1	0	2	0
P	2	0	0	0	1	0	0	2	0	0	0	0	26	18	6	11	1	7	2	27	0	1	0

CLEANING USE

Benefit Deficiency

The mainstream of the analysis, dealing with benefits and attributes, begins by examining how much each of the benefits is both *wanted* and *received*. This is done by summing ratings across all respondents and across all cleaning occasions. Figure 8.3 shows a benefit deficiency matrix for one specific benefit: removes grease. Marginal totals show the extent to which removing grease was both *wanted* and *received* by housewives on the following scale:

4 = wanted (received) a lot

3 = wanted (received) pretty much

2 = wanted (received) somewhat

1 = didn't want (receive) at all

Thus, 196 of the 500 respondents said they wanted to remove grease "a whole lot," 143 said "not at all." The frequencies for "received" are similar. However, simple comparisons of marginal frequencies obscure *the extent to which specific benefits are wanted but not received.*

For example, 34 respondents said they wanted to remove grease "a whole lot" but the cleaning product they used did so "not at all," a rather impressive need-deficiency score of 3 (4 - 1). Another 26 wanted to remove grease "a whole lot" but their product did so only "somewhat," and 23 wanted this "pretty much" and got it "not at all"—for a total of 49 respondents with a need-deficiency score of 2. An additional 79 respondents had a need-deficiency score of 1, making a total of 162 of the 500 respondents with some perceived deficiency in the removal of grease—almost exactly one third of the sample! While some of the 79 deficiency scores of 1 should be discounted because of the basic unreliability of any such survey data, there still appears to exist a rather sizable segment of respondents who were not satisfied with the grease-removal properties of the cleaning compounds they used.

Figure 8.3

BENEFIT DEFICIENCY MATRIX

Benefit No. 49: "Removes grease"						
Received:	"Not at all"	"Somewhat"	"Pretty much"	"A Whole lot"	Marginal Sums	
Wanted					Wanted	Received
"A whole lot"	34	26	27	109	196	147
"Pretty much"	23	30	25	20	98	75
"Somewhat"	22	15	13	6	56	84
"Not at all"	108	13	10	12	143	187
TOTAL:	187	84	75	147		

Averages: Wanted: 2.70   Received: 2.36

Want minus Received =	−3	−2	−1	0	1	2	3	Average deficiency = .335
No. of Respondents:[a]	12	16	46	257	79	49	34	

Avg. positive deficiency = .566   Avg. negative deficiency = .231
Proportion with deficiency = .329   Proportion with negative deficiency = .150
Proportion want 3+ with deficiency = .284   Proportion want 2− with negative deficiency = .110

[a]Totals include different combinations of "Want minus Received."

"Deficiency indexes" can be calculated from these data in a number of ways:

1. *Average deficiency.* This is a simple weighted average of both positive (wanted but not received) and negative (received but not wanted) deficiencies.

2. *Average positive deficiency.* Since most *benefit* statements are worded in the affirmative (something potentially desirable), positive deficiencies would normally be much more important than negative ones. An average positive deficiency index can be calculated by ignoring negative deficiencies (setting them equal to zero) and recalculating the weighted average deficiency, which more accurately reflects the extent to which the subjects wanted a particular benefit but did not get it.

3. *Proportion with deficiency.* The above weighted averages are useful in later plots, but they do not communicate very meaningful information to management. The proportion of the sample with some specified deficiency (1 or more, 2 or more, etc.) is intrinsically much clearer and is easily calculated.

4. *Proportion wanting 3+ with deficiency.* Even more meaningful might be the proportion *of those who wanted the benefit 3 (pretty much) or more* who had a deficiency of some specified size.

All of these deficiency indexes are shown in Figure 8.3 for the "removes grease" benefit.

Similar deficiencies can be calculated for each of the product characteristics; however, the situation here is quite different from that for benefits. Since product characteristics are *neutral* (i.e., purely descriptive) whereas most benefits are (usually) *positive,* deficiency indexes for the former should be both positive and negative— the latter reflecting the extent to which a particular characteristic was received but not wanted. Thus, the following additional deficiency indexes can be calculated:

5. *Average negative deficiency.* This is derived by setting all positive deficiencies equal to zero and calculating a weighted average negative deficiency.

6. *Proportion with negative deficiency.* This represents the proportion of all respondents having a negative deficiency of 1 or more (or 2 or more, if desired), indicating that they received the characteristic more than they wanted it.

7. *Proportion wanting 2- with deficiency.* This represents the proportion of all respondents wanting a characteristic only "some-

121

what" or "not at all" who received that characteristic more than they wanted it.

The above calculations are shown in Figure 8.3 for the *benefit* "removes grease" (even though negative deficiencies would not normally be used for benefits but only for characteristics since benefits are always positive, by definition). In the analysis, a benefit deficiency matrix is prepared for each *product characteristic* as well, using the same format.

Plots of Benefits Wanted vs. Deficiencies

While the above information provides useful diagnostics for each benefit (or characteristic), it needs to be organized and summarized [in a more meaningful fashion] for the market planner. Plotting benefits (characteristics) wanted versus deficiencies is a simple yet useful first step.

Using benefits to illustrate, several possible plots would be meaningful: (1) benefits wanted versus received; (2) benefits wanted versus average positive deficiency; (3) benefits wanted versus proportion with some deficiency; (4) benefits wanted versus proportion wanting the benefit "pretty much" or more with some deficiency.

Figure 8.4 shows a plot of average benefit wanted scores versus average positive deficiency scores for each of the 80 benefits respondents wanted from household cleaning products. Wanted scores are positioned vertically,[2] deficiency scores horizontally. The reader can see at a glance those benefits that are:

—Wanted most but are not deficient (none in this example)

—Wanted most and are moderately deficient (nos. 44, 71, 72)

—Wanted most and are quite deficient (nos. 10, 60)

—Wanted moderately and are quite deficient (nos. 22, 38, 51)

The dotted lines enclose benefits that are similar and are in the same benefit grouping, as will be discussed in the next section of this chapter.

---

[2]Note the maximum and minimum values of Y at the bottom of the plot; these are average wanted scores on the four-point scale (4 = wanted a whole lot; 1 = not wanted at all). The same is true for deficiency scores on the X axis.

122

Figure 8.4

PLOT OF BENEFITS WANTED VERSUS DEFICIENCIES

AVERAGE BENEFIT WANTED

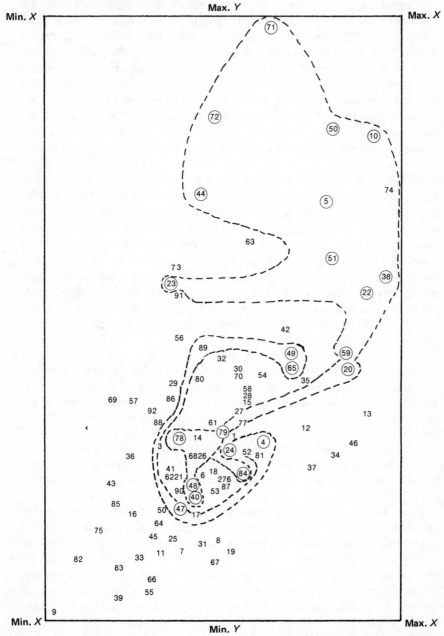

Minimum Value of X = .070
Maximum Value of X = .410

AVERAGE POSITIVE DEFICIENCY
Minimum Value of Y = 1.170
Maximum Value of Y = 3.160

The plot enables rapid identification of opportunity areas on which to focus further diagnostic and planning efforts. While this particular plot does not show any spectacular deficiency points (in the sense that the most wanted benefit[s] was not the most deficient one), it does show moderate deficiencies for some highly wanted benefits and serious deficiencies for some that were wanted to a moderate degree. The latter often constitute one or more respondent segments that are particularly sensitive to some needs that are not adequately met by presently available products (e.g., strong cleaning power that does not irritate the hands, an all-purpose stain remover that is easy to apply, an inexpensive product for a variety of light cleaning uses, a special product for cleaning refrigerators).

The plot in Figure 8.4 portrays the entire cleaning products market. Information that is even more useful is often gained from similar plots for each *product type* (16) and for each *cleaning use* (23) separately. Such plots often show two or three product types (or uses) that are particularly vulnerable because they are not adequately meeting some needs that are wanted highly or even moderately. Carefully designed new product entries could be expected to compete effectively in these product areas *because they are specifically targeted at benefits people say they want a great deal but are not now getting.* (One proprietary study clearly revealed the existence of such gaps for three major product types.)

It is important to note that the less a particular benefit is wanted, the less chance it has to register a large deficiency. Something a respondent wants only somewhat (scale value of 2) can only have a deficiency of 1; something wanted a whole lot (scale value of 4) can have a deficiency of as much as 3. This means that benefits wanted only moderately but with large deficiencies are probably severely deficient for those people who did want them, suggesting segments that should be particularly promising for the right new product entry.

Plots for product characteristics proceed in the same fashion as for benefits, with one important additional type of plot. Since particular characteristics *may or may not* be wanted, plots of average *negative* deficiencies versus characteristics received (rather than wanted) reveal quickly those characteristics that are received when they are not wanted (e.g., strong aroma, grittiness). This information can be used to remove unwanted specific characteristics from existing products, if this is technically feasible; if such action is not feasible, this information might suggest an entirely new approach to certain cleaning needs or to cleaning products.

Overall Benefit and Deficiency Structure

The next step is to construct a benefit and deficiency structure graph for the household cleaning products market, *on an aggregate basis,* as shown in Figure 8.5. This graph says that the primary benefits people want from cleaning products fall into seven major groupings, labeled A ("removes dust/dirt/film") through G ("gentle on hands/skin").

These benefit dimensions are produced by grouping together specific benefits *wanted* that are perceived as similar. This is done by clustering (using any one of several clustering techniques) all 80 benefit wanted ratings across all respondents and all cleaning occasions. The problem here is that clustering techniques in general do not even consider the relative importance of each of the various benefits wanted; they merely perform an exercise in semantics, by grouping benefit descriptions that are seen as similar by respondents (in terms of the extent to which they want each of these benefits).

What is needed is a technique that simultaneously *groups* and *weights* the benefits in rank order of frequency desired. If one or more benefits wanted a great deal is in fact an "isolate"—that is, not perceived as similar to any other benefit—the technique used must identify isolates as well as groupings. Presumably the desired technique would be sequential, extracting first the benefit or benefit cluster wanted most, then the one wanted next most, and so on until all of the most important benefits were accounted for.

Unfortunately, to our knowledge no such technique has yet been developed.[3] The best current alternative is to judgmentally do something like the following:

1. Place benefits in rank order on the basis of their average benefit wanted score. This can be done in the form of listings of averages or, better still, by using the aggregate *plot* of benefits wanted versus benefits received.

---

[3]The reader may wonder why the "factor analysis of weighted covariances" technique discussed in Chapter 4 could not be used here. Remember that the data available for the more restrictive type of positioning described in that chapter included a *dependent variable* (e.g., overall evaluations, buying intention ratings, actual choice among competing alternatives). Such a dependent variable is simply not available in the typical benefit structure analysis study.

Figure 8.5

BENEFIT AND DEFICIENCY STRUCTURE GRAPH
FOR CLEANING PRODUCTS

Major Benefit Grouping

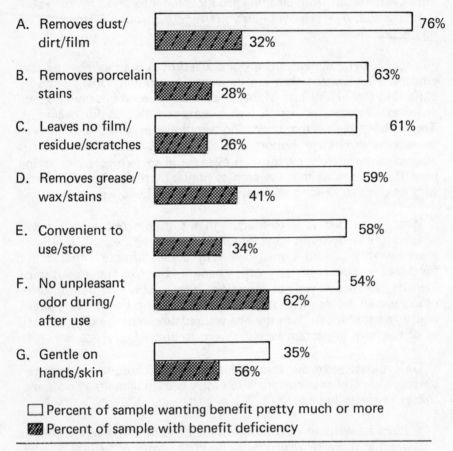

A. Removes dust/dirt/film — 76% / 32%

B. Removes porcelain stains — 63% / 28%

C. Leaves no film/residue/scratches — 61% / 26%

D. Removes grease/wax/stains — 59% / 41%

E. Convenient to use/store — 58% / 34%

F. No unpleasant odor during/after use — 54% / 62%

G. Gentle on hands/skin — 35% / 56%

☐ Percent of sample wanting benefit pretty much or more
▨ Percent of sample with benefit deficiency

2. Using the latter, circle the top benefit (with the highest benefit wanted score) in a selected color.

3. Find the benefit with the second highest wanted score. Using a cluster analysis of all 80 benefits, see if this benefit falls *primarily* in the same factor or cluster as the top benefit. If so, circle it with the same color and draw a line connecting the two. If not, circle the second benefit with another color and proceed to the third most wanted benefit.

4. Follow this procedure through all 80 benefits, from top to bottom, connecting individual benefits that fall in the same grouping of benefits on the basis of the factor analysis or clustering procedure.

5. Each resulting benefit cluster forms one of the seven "major benefit groupings" shown in Figure 8.5.

6. The relative size for each benefit grouping is determined by: (a) using the average benefit wanted score of the single benefit in the grouping (or the isolate) wanted most: or (b) counting the number of respondents wanting this key "marker" benefit "pretty much" or a "whole lot"; or (c) developing some sort of weighted average wanted score using all the benefits in the cluster, the top 5 or 10 benefits, or something similar.

Deficiencies for each of these benefit structure dimensions are developed in a manner parallel to that used for amount wanted and are juxtaposed on the same graph. The final graph shows at a glance the benefit and deficiency structure of the household cleaning products market. The exact same analysis should be done for *product characteristics,* to develop a market structure in these terms.

Benefit Linkages

Products deliver *combinations* of benefits; no product has only a single benefit. The next step in the analysis is to link each of the benefit wanted dimensions (or product characteristic dimensions) with all others, to provide a view of the relative potential for building new products containing *two* or more benefits or features people want.

There are several ways to build linkages. The simplest one that yields meaningful data is to choose some key marker variable to represent each benefit structure dimension; this would normally be the single benefit wanted most.[4] Each of the seven markers is then linked with every other one to produce 21 pairs of both benefits and deficiencies. Graphs of these linkages can be prepared and put in some meaningful rank order for easier comparison. The graphs show both *number* and *percentage* of all respondents who:

---

[4]Another approach would be to weight all benefits within a dimension cluster to produce a composite score for that dimension. This raises the question of what the weights should be based on: cluster "fit" indexes (e.g., factor loadings if factor analysis is used), average benefit wanted indexes, or some other measure.

1. Want both benefits "pretty much" (3) or "a whole lot" (4)

2. Want both benefits "a whole lot" (4)

3. Have a deficiency of 1 or more on both benefits

4. Want both benefits "pretty much" or more *and* have a deficiency or 1 or more on both

5. Have a deficiency of 2 or more on both benefits

Any number of other combinations is possible (e.g., number and percentage wanting both benefits pretty much or more who have a deficiency of 2 or more on *either*). Large benefit wanted linkages with large deficiencies can be quickly spotted, as can be smaller ones with large deficiencies. The latter often signal market segments that offer real promise for some new product, or for the repositioning of some existing product.

Ideal Cleaning Product

Extension of the above linkages into three benefits at a time yields very meager numbers of respondents wanting each combination "pretty much" or more. The best that can be done is to choose (subjectively) any *three* of the major benefit dimensions wanted, to use as the axes of a three-dimensional positioning map. The benefits selected might be the top three in rank order, or it may be more useful to select from among the top four or five. For example, "convenience" is often among the top three features wanted for many products, yet it is frequently an entirely different type of consideration from other major benefit dimensions (e.g., food chemistry in the case of a food product) and might be dealt with by developmental labs on a different basis.

Once the dimensions have been chosen, average benefit *received* scores for each of the cleaning products can be determined and plotted in the usual fashion. Benefit received averages can be obtained from the single marker variable for each dimension or from some weighted average of received scores on the various benefits making up each major benefit dimension.

The resulting three-dimensional configuration should be considered a *preference* map, similar to those constructed by factor analysis of weighted covariances (see Chapter 4) or by nonmetric scaling of some form of preference matrix or of rank orders of preference. The map can be used to evaluate present product/service offerings, to find promising gaps in the market that offer opportunities for new product development, to reposition existing products through promotion efforts, to improve present products, and the like.

As an aside, in several studies involving three-dimensional preference positioning of products (e.g., small cars, motorcycles, orange-juice-type drinks), we have yet to find a single product that is clearly closest to the "ideal"—a hypothetical product perceived to contain maximum amounts of the three benefits or features people want most. A few products will be fairly high on two of the three dimensions but will have only moderate or even low ratings on the third. Implications for product improvement are often obvious.

Relationship of Benefits and Characteristics

Up to this point, emphasis has been placed largely on benefits. But once it is determined what benefits and combinations of benefits are wanted, how are these benefits produced? A benefit structure study shows, at a minimum, what *types of product characteristics* are seen by respondents as being most closely associated with any single benefit or any group of related benefits. This provides a linkage between benefits and the product characteristics that produce those benefits.

While this can be done in several ways, the simplest is to correlate benefit *received* scores with product characteristic *received* scores, across all respondents and cleaning occasions. Since both are measured on the same four-point interval scale, the sizes of the correlations should be quite meaningful in identifying which characteristics are most likely and which are least likely to produce the benefit.

In one recent study, though, no correlation exceeded .23, indicating a rather low relationship. We have seldom found any in excess of .40; most linkages show highest correlations in the .30s. This makes the job of the new product planner more difficult, in that relationships are not high enough to *clearly* indicate what product characteristics should be used to produce a given benefit. Still, comparisons of those relating highest with those relating lowest usually indicate clear differences in the general *types* of characteristics that are and are not perceived to be related to a particular benefit.

129

Sometimes such relationships are obvious and predictable *a priori.* For example, the removal of "heavy" dirt and grease would normally require a "strong" cleaning compound. But should the new product be cloudy or clear? Thick or thin? Dark or light? (In the context of developing a new food product, what is a "fancy" food like? Or beverage that is "fun" or "good for the soul"?) At least some of these questions can be answered by the correlations of benefits with product characteristics.

If none of the relationships is high (perhaps .30 or more), this would suggest that the planner is free to use any product characteristics he chooses, since nothing is especially strongly related to the particular benefit under study across *all* products and respondents. On the other hand, if removers of heavy dirt and/or grease are perceived more often to be a dark paste, the planner should know that he probably faces a more difficult selling job with a milky liquid.

A more technically satisfying way of linking benefits and characteristics would be to factor analyze (or cluster in some way) both types of items and then correlate the benefit factor scores against characteristic factor scores. This yields a tidier solution that can be very useful in simplifying things for the planner. On the other hand, it can also obscure meaningful relationships for specific benefits that might provide especially useful clues during the laborious heuristic process any planner must follow in working from data to get clearly defined new product ideas. The answer is to do both types of analysis if time and budget are available.

Relationships of Benefits and Products

In a manner parallel to linking benefits with *characteristics,* benefits can be linked to *products* to show what types of products are considered best at delivering each of the 80 benefits. One useful approach is to rank order all product categories (sixteen in the present study) in terms of their average benefit *received* scores for each benefit.

Note that these averages are based only on the numbers of respondents using each product type on the single randomly selected cleaning occasion. There is no assurance that these groups are parallel. (Respondents tending to use certain product types might be more enthusiastic raters than others, or they might be more critical. There is some evidence of this from one of our studies.) Still, the resulting rankings have been found to be quite useful in indicating the general types of products that are most (and least) likely to produce any specific benefit.

Simultaneous Row/Column Linkages

Up to this point, all benefit linkages have been done one at a time, in a sense, and the resulting data are more diagnostic than structural. The same general types of information can be presented in a form that provides greater overall structure to the market at the same time that it allows specific diagnostic information, but in a different format. This is done using a process that groups and displays two variables simultaneously. The reader will recall that this type of analysis was used by Stefflre (see Chapter 7, Figures 7.1 and 7.2). The simultaneous row/column clustering algorithm used in the benefit structure study reported here was developed by Dr. Edward W. Forgy[4] and named LARC (large row/column simultaneous clustering). LARC is applied to data aggregated across groups of respondents—normally *all* respondents in a study.

Table 8.4 shows a row/column linkage analysis of cleaning occasions (columns) with benefits wanted (rows). Cleaning occasions that are seen as similar in terms of benefits wanted are grouped together, as are benefits that are seen as similar in terms of cleaning uses.

The LARC process begins by summing benefit wanted scores (from 1 to 4) over all respondents for each cleaning need separately and for each benefit separately. These numbers are the entries in Table 8.4. They are first summed to get marginal totals for both rows and columns; then rows and columns are independently rank ordered in terms of these marginal totals.

The grouping process is sequential and begins at any specified point, usually with the most frequent benefit (or use). The next most frequent one is then selected and some form of index of similarity of the two rows (or columns) is calculated.[5] The next most frequent row is selected and a similarities index between this and each of the other two is calculated. The computer algorithm then selects the

---

[4]Statistical consultant, Los Angeles, California.

[5]There are several possibilities based on difference scores ("distances") between rows. We have used both. Sim. = 1-D/2; Sim. = 1/D + 1, where D is the sum of the differences between corresponding entries in the matrix, across rows/columns.

proper location for the third row on the basis of (1) a comparison of the similarities indexes and (2) an overall index of similarity between all rows combined (this index is to be maximized).

Following this process the computer first groups rows, then columns, then displays both rows and columns simultaneously, as in Table 8.4. This exhibit shows market structure more clearly by indicating: (1) groups of similar cleaning needs for which groups of similar benefits (or even some isolate benefits) are desired, and (2) groups of cleaning needs that are seen as most appropriate for a given group of similar benefits (or isolates). Boxes have been formed somewhat arbitrarily around the largest blocks of numbers to show the most clearly defined linkages.

It is important to note that LARC or any similar process *will not define clusters of rows or columns as clearly and accurately as will the various algorithms that are designed solely for clustering.* However, this weakness is compensated for by the ability of a LARC-type analysis to both group *and* display simultaneously linkages between the two variables under study.

Row/column analysis should be done for benefits *received* and benefit *deficiencies* in addition to benefits wanted. The study of benefit deficiencies by product and by cleaning use is often particularly helpful. Likewise, a row/column analysis of products by cleaning uses should also be done; this produces basically the same information as the Stefflre "item-use" matrix and has the advantage of being aggregated over all respondents rather than providing separate matrices for each.

To summarize, several types of row/column analysis should be done:

1. Products by cleaning use

2. Products by *benefits* wanted, received, deficiencies

3. Cleaning uses by benefits wanted, received, deficiencies

4. Products by *characteristics* wanted, received, deficiencies

5. Cleaning uses by characteristics wanted, received, deficiencies

Table 8.4

ROW/COLUMN LINKAGE ANALYSIS FOR CLEANING PRODUCTS

Cleaning Occasion	Freq.	Benefits Wanted																				
		18	3	13	19	2	6	12	21	1	7	9	17	10	20	16	8	4	11	5	15	14
2	716	127	104	74	76	11	19	9	20	37	34	12	9	6	4	4	5	3	2	77	44	39
28	540	95	68	49	49	18	12	7	15	22	21	7	8	5	5	8	4	5	4	61	35	42
32	416	79	66	41	45	9	10	6	8	18	12	7	9	4	6	4	7	3	3	40	20	19
4	852	39	44	47	41	40	41	43	43	37	37	39	36	36	33	35	35	32	33	44	53	66
12	108	5	8	8	7	4	4	3	4	6	8	3	6	4	4	8	6	4	5	2	3	6
50	140	6	4	7	7	11	10	9	8	7	7	8	10	5	6	7	6	5	4	5	3	5
22	197	7	8	7	11	6	4	9	11	14	14	6	13	11	9	12	12	16	16	1	3	7
8	190	6	8	11	10	9	9	5	9	12	16	6	8	7	7	12	11	11	7	4	10	12
47	211	11	13	10	12	9	7	13	13	12	11	8	11	7	12	9	8	11	6	11	8	9
37	230	13	18	14	11	11	14	12	16	12	14	8	13	9	13	8	7	11	7	9	4	6
49	257	11	12	11	12	10	19	17	21	14	17	11	12	10	14	12	14	11	8	5	6	10
30	282	12	10	12	15	9	14	15	18	19	16	14	16	14	13	11	12	15	15	10	12	10
19	286	10	14	18	11	11	12	19	16	17	12	11	18	16	20	13	16	16	13	6	9	8
51	333	10	10	16	24	41	19	18	16	12	14	15	14	13	17	20	20	17	13	6	7	11
39	352	10	5	16	22	46	21	20	18	16	18	15	18	17	17	19	15	18	14	8	8	11
21	369	14	21	21	15	33	22	25	26	26	17	18	17	10	11	12	13	8	5	22	17	16
13	353	19	24	20	15	19	23	27	24	29	18	14	22	12	13	6	7	9	8	19	14	11
36	284	10	22	18	11	5	21	22	26	25	17	21	17	10	11	5	5	8	7	10	8	5
41	332	10	18	10	11	10	39	33	33	21	22	30	24	19	6	5	9	10	12	4	3	3
44	460	14	10	17	18	20	44	40	38	30	35	47	33	29	13	12	16	15	18	3	3	5
10	512	11	17	17	19	18	52	48	46	38	42	43	39	29	15	15	14	19	18	5	4	5
7	594	24	28	36	39	16	43	45	47	38	40	40	37	30	19	20	17	20	23	6	11	15
26	520	23	30	33	36	18	34	42	45	34	38	31	33	24	18	10	15	14	21	6	7	10
33	506	31	36	32	32	15	33	38	37	34	30	35	31	27	17	12	14	19	18	5	5	5
34	508	30	30	31	27	25	27	26	28	29	25	25	21	21	20	16	17	21	23	15	19	32
48	518	21	24	23	25	29	40	28	32	29	31	30	25	25	23	24	21	23	20	17	13	15
20	560	16	12	20	34	66	35	31	24	31	33	27	27	27	21	29	33	30	27	9	11	17
17	562	11	12	20	38	75	31	29	24	29	28	25	27	26	24	26	31	36	25	12	14	19
9	515	13	18	22	19	20	24	24	21	22	25	27	25	31	30	40	30	32	36	10	26	20
40	544	20	23	31	21	14	13	25	24	31	24	23	28	32	32	31	34	35	37	11	36	19
42	494	21	23	24	20	14	20	24	26	25	25	21	25	23	28	27	27	27	29	20	20	24
29	454	17	17	23	15	16	14	14	15	18	20	20	20	32	34	31	31	30	31	23	17	16
43	424	12	16	15	16	15	14	15	19	23	16	22	24	33	29	36	34	33	36	2	8	6
5	408	18	21	14	15	13	22	20	17	14	17	22	28	30	31	28	27	28	27	5	6	5
45	373	21	19	15	16	15	12	11	12	17	18	16	14	21	24	29	31	25	28	10	11	10
23	357	13	17	14	19	11	14	9	8	10	16	17	13	19	18	20	26	20	21	31	22	22
6	295	6	6	3	7	12	11	7	5	8	15	13	18	21	22	29	22	23	25	18	19	19
31	250	10	8	8	9	12	6	6	5	7	6	10	11	10	19	22	22	21	22	11	14	11
15	233	8	8	8	9	18	5	8	7	8	7	6	11	10	24	22	17	18	15	5	6	13
14	235	12	12	16	10	16	6	8	7	8	10	8	11	8	11	19	12	13	10	14	13	13
35	236	13	5	10	10	9	8	10	8	11	12	12	10	14	14	15	12	14	12	14	14	13
25	372	10	10	11	11	12	8	15	10	13	12	17	20	25	30	25	23	28	30	20	25	17
3	395	15	16	20	14	12	5	15	16	19	15	11	17	18	27	29	24	24	30	6	37	25
24	458	16	19	17	16	27	14	19	18	23	17	13	19	21	27	24	29	28	17	38	30	26
38	439	8	10	11	13	23	10	15	12	12	10	16	20	21	31	22	26	24	21	33	45	56
16	632	18	15	21	27	34	46	35	31	21	39	43	33	30	27	27	29	26	28	33	35	34
46	570	24	29	27	27	35	16	14	17	23	25	19	17	20	24	29	23	22	22	51	48	58
18	592	23	15	14	13	24	20	13	14	15	22	25	20	29	30	33	27	29	36	65	60	65
27	583	16	12	16	13	26	19	21	17	14	14	30	24	36	41	33	34	35	37	53	47	46
11	668	17	15	19	13	24	27	25	19	19	27	36	30	40	36	41	42	41	48	51	57	41
1	824	19	17	27	17	28	31	35	30	24	21	40	38	55	47	48	45	47	57	72	77	49

Note: Data ordered by row column similarities based on 493 respondents.

6. Benefits/characteristics wanted, received, and deficiencies by such other questionnaire information as demographics, psychographics, brand, usage volume, and the like, as available

Row/column simultaneous clustering provides a highly useful form of market structure for the market planner. He or she can spot at a glance which general types of cleaning needs require which general types of benefits or product characteristics. The planner can also trace the size of the corresponding deficiencies to locate the more promising avenues for new product ideas. Previous analyses (e.g., plots) contain some of the same information but on a more fragmented basis—for each product or cleaning need separately, or for each benefit or characteristic separately.

Row/column clustering deals with the entire fabric of products and benefits simultaneously. Yet it also enables the planner to isolate a specific product or cleaning need he is most interested in and to trace this to see the degree to which it relates to any one or all of the benefits or product characteristics. Conversely, he can trace any specific benefit in terms of the products in which it is most likely to be found, or the cleaning uses for which it is most desired. Experience from studies to date shows that the product planner will pore over LARCs for hours, tracing products, cleaning uses, benefits, characteristics, and various specific deficiencies.

Additional Analyses

There are many additional analyses that should be useful for the market planner. For example, those respondents who most wanted a particular cleaning benefit *or* characteristic can be sorted out and compared to the total sample in terms of demographics, time of day, and other questionnaire data not included in previous analyses (one firm asked for mental and physical "feeling tone," plus limited psychographics). It is also possible to greatly expand the number of specific benefit (characteristic) pairs to get relationships other than those from the selected key marker benefits for a particular cluster.

Another useful analysis consists of isolating those respondents who most wanted a particular benefit (or benefit cluster, using factor scores) and determining the following averages for each *product characteristic*: (1) average wanted score, (2) average received score, (3) average positive deficiency score, and (4) average negative deficiency score. Comparison of these averages shows what characteristics are particularly crucial for a given benefit or benefit cluster. This can also be done by correlation analysis, as reported earlier, but in a different format.

ADVANTAGES AND LIMITATIONS

A benefit structure analysis study has several advantages:

1. It enables the systematic study of consumer satisfactions and unmet needs in *broadly defined* product categories, such as uses of money, communications needs, and recreational pursuits. While a number of the approaches discussed earlier do this to some extent, they provide far less specific diagnostic information than a benefit structure analysis study.

2. It constitutes a vast data bank relating products, characteristics, benefits, product characteristics, and other types of information included in the particular study questionnaire. These data are used not only for the principal analyses described earlier, but they also answer a wide variety of lesser questions dealing with such factors as time of day, "situation" surrounding the use of a product, tracing of selected benefits/products/uses, and the like.

3. A single study provides many different forms of market structure. In this sense, it is more similar to the Stefflre process than to any of the previous forms of structural analysis discussed in this book.

4. Benefit structure analysis provides both *structural* and *diagnostic* types of information. It can be used to "structure" either the entire market or some portion thereof (e.g., kitchen cleaning) by showing benefits/characteristics wanted, received, and deficiencies, as well as various linkages. It provides "diagnostic" information by enabling the researcher to select, say, a single product or cleaning use and look closely for actionable deficiencies therein.

5. Results from this type of study are easier to communicate to management since they are based on simple answers to simple questions; also, most of the analytic procedures are conceptually simpler than most of the procedures discussed in earlier chapters.

A benefit structure study is not without limitations however:

1. Such a study requires about one hour of time and concentration from a respondent. This is a great deal to ask, and the usual problems of respondent fatigue in any survey interview are intensified in this type of study. The resulting data are likely to be less reliable than would be desired.

2. There is no assurance that preliminary focus group and depth interviews have brought out *all* of the most important benefits/characteristics for the general product/service category under study.

3. There emerge the usual questions about the accuracy of interval scales for the data in this study. Since all data manipulations are based on additions and subtractions of scaled data, metric assumptions may be more important for a benefit structure study than for most others. As a precautionary measure, the scale statements (a whole lot, pretty much, somewhat, not at all) were selected using Thurstone's equal-interval scaling technique. This should produce scales that are at least close to interval.

4. This type of study merely represents a systematic way of asking people directly what they want and what some of their unfilled needs are. It rests on the assumption that people are both *willing* and *able* to give such information in response to direct questioning. There is always some doubt as to whether they can do so. In contrast, other approaches discussed in earlier chapters do not usually rely on direct questioning to such a degree.

5. The problem of product *availability* may be important. It is very likely that some of the "deficiencies" in benefits and characteristics reported by respondents are due only to the fact that the product desired was not immediately available in the home when the cleaning took place. The extent of this problem can be estimated by including a question or two in the data gathering phase (e.g., "What product would you have used *if* you could have used anything you wanted?" Also, "What *other* products would have been suitable?").

On balance, benefit structure analysis is one more tool for structuring markets in a way that is particularly useful for new product planning. It appears to provide more *specific* information about benefits wanted and benefit deficiencies than any of the techniques we have discussed thus far. Therefore, it can be a useful adjunct to other research techniques employed by the market planner.

REFERENCES TO CHAPTER 8

1. Myers, James H. "Benefit Structure Analysis: A New Tool for Product Planning, " *Journal of Marketing,* 40 (October 1976), 23-32.

Chapter 9

CONJOINT MEASUREMENT
(MULTIPLE TRADE-OFF ANALYSIS)

However illuminating all of the preceding "models" or approaches might be, they share at least one problem. Green observes: "What appears to be missing . . . are descriptions of how *any* of the models propose to transform psychological dimensions—actionable or not—into 'objective' dimensions. Moreover, the converse problem of predicting psychological response to physical changes in stimuli is also far from trivial and, indeed, is not treated in any of the models." [1, p. 27]

To illustrate the problem, suppose a positioning map (either perceptual or preference) for bar soaps suggests that consumers might want a soap that is more "fragrant" than any of the existing best sellers. What does this mean to the market planner? *How much* more fragrant? What *kind* of fragrance—lemon, floral, medicinal?

One of the present authors developed a preference map for an existing type of fruit drink which suggested that "mouth feel" was the most important feature in consumer evaluations of this type of drink. What does the term *mouth feel* mean, in the language of the food chemist who must produce a better fruit drink? Does it have more plup? Alum? Ascorbic acid? A higher brix-acid ratio? Or does it have less of one or more of these? And how *much* more or less *in terms of a scale on some laboratory measuring instrument?*

Ideal Product

A concept developed by researchers who specialize in positioning studies is the "ideal" product. Previous chapters have described how an ideal point might be identified within a perceptual or preference map. However, a product that might be considered by a consumer as ideal in terms of the best combination of levels of various attributes or benefits might not be feasible or even possible to construct. For example, the ideal car for one person might have the gas economy of a Volkswagen, the interior room of a Cadillac, the handling of a Corvette, and the price of a Honda! While the concept is nice, technological considerations make such a car impossible. Thus, in the real world consumers often cannot have their ideal product and instead are forced to *trade off* some features for others.

Economists believe that consumers have "utility functions" that cause them to select a particular product or brand on the basis of the relative importance they place on each of its various attributes. Different consumers usually have different utility functions; otherwise market segments would not exist and all consumers would prefer one product (combination of attribute levels). Trade-off analysis, also called conjoint analysis, is a technique to determine for each consumer: (1) the relative importance of each of the various attributes a given type of product is composed of, (2) the desirability of each "level" or condition of each attribute, and (3) the optimum *combination of attribute levels or conditions* into a "package" (product) that is most ideal, within price and technological constraints. *Trade-off analysis is most appropriate for product categories where consumers would like as much of each level of an attribute as they can get but where constraints (usually cost) force them to make trade-offs.*

A variety of procedures have been developed to derive consumers' utility functions for attributes and levels of attributes [see 2, 3, 4, 6]. The two approaches currently used most widely (orthogonal arrays and pair-wise trade-off comparisons) are discussed below.

PROCEDURE

A trade-off analysis (conjoint measurement) study requires several steps:

1. A list of product attributes considered relevant to the category is prepared.

2. Various levels or conditions of each attribute are defined.

3. An experimental design is selected that will provide various *combinations* of these levels or conditions that will be presented to consumers. These combinations provide the basis for "trade-off" judgments.

4. A sample of respondents is asked to *rank order their choices of these combinations of attribute levels.*

5. A statistical technique is applied to each individual's rank-ordered choices in order to develop his particular utility function, that is, the relative value he places on each level or condition of each attribute. These utilities are calculated to account as closely as possible for the overall preference ranks.

6. A market simulation model is developed to "predict" what choices each individual will make in the marketplace, given his utility functions and the existing alternative products available, as defined by the levels or conditions of attributes each product provides.

Each of these steps is discussed below.

Selection of Product Attributes

First, "relevant" product attributes must be identified. For example, in a study by Green and Wind [4] concerning a spot remover and cleaner for carpets and upholstery, management selected five product attributes: type of applicator package, brand name, price, existence of the *Good Housekeeping* seal of approval, and money-back guarantee. Whether this list includes all the most important attributes that consumers consider in choosing among spot removers remains to be seen; clearly, management judgment may be near-sighted in omitting relevant features.

Defining Attribute Levels or Conditions

The second step involves selecting a number of levels or conditions for each feature. Sometimes there are only two levels—a product either has the Good Housekeeping seal or it does not. Often, however, attributes are continuous variables, such as price. Sometimes attributes are discrete but possess no ordinal properties, such as type of applicator. The levels of each attribute are generally chosen by judgment. It is wise to include a range of alternative levels (e.g., on price) that would encompass all possible product brands in the market; however, both the experimental design selected and consumer fatigue in evaluation pragmatically limit the number of levels for any one attribute.

Combinations of Attribute Levels

Constructing a list of combinations of the attribute levels to present to consumers is handled differently by various researchers. Green and Wind use a special *factorial design* (called an orthogonal array) in which the test combinations are selected so that the independent contributions of all five factors are balanced. Each factor's weight is kept separate and is not confused with those of the other factors [4]. Thus, each combination presented to a respondent contains only *one level* of *all* the attributes under consideration, so each combination represents an entire product "package."

Johnson approaches this step differently [6]. He presents respondents with a larger list of *pairs* of each level of each attribute against each level of every other attribute. For example, Table 9.1 presents one respondent's trade-off judgments for various pairs of levels of four attributes of automobiles: price, top speed, seating capacity, and months of warranty. The number of combinations a respondent must rank is generally higher using this method, but he need consider only a single pair of attributes at a time (e.g., price $2,500, top speed 130 m.p.h.).

Both of these approaches make the same basic assumption: no "interaction" effects. It is assumed that no synergistic effects (positive or negative) occur when any *particular combination* of attribute levels is offered. For many product categories this simply may not be true. As Johnson suggests: "The model assumes, for instance, that the extent to which a respondent prefers a red car to a black one will be independent of size, price and model type. It seems possible that red may be someone's preferred color for a convertible and black would be preferred for a limousine." [6, p. 124]

Researchers who have conducted preference experiments with food know that "first order" (and sometimes higher) interaction effects do in fact occur. Often the most significant new product ideas come about from the synergistic effects of two attributes, individual-

Table 9.1

ONE RESPONDENT'S TRADE-OFF DATA
(RANK ORDERS OF PREFERENCE)

	Top Speed			Seating capacity			Months of warranty	
	130	100	70	2	4	6	60	12
Price								
$2,500	1	2	5	2	1	3	1	3
$4,000	3	4	5	5	4	6	2	5
$6,000	7	8	9	8	7	9	7	8
Top speed								
130 MPH				2	1	3	1	2
100 MPH				5	4	6	3	4
70 MPH				8	7	9	7	8
Seating capacity								
2							3	5
4							1	4
6							3	6

Source: Johnson [6].

ly not very significant, but combined in a new way to produce something very desirable. For example, bringing together the *food form* of a "tart" and the *preparation method* of a toaster yielded the successful toaster Pop-tart breakfast food. (One method of idea generation is based on this notion of synergism of attributes [9].) In spite of this rather limiting assumption, trade-off studies have proved useful when interaction effects can be assumed to be negligible or nonexistent.

Consumer Evaluations

The next step is to submit a list of the various combinations of attributes to consumers for their evaluation. The simplest method is to ask a target segment of consumers to rank order the list, using instructions such as: "Please look at each of these descriptions for various features of product category. Place them in the order that you would be most likely to buy them in the marketplace." Using the

Figure 9.1

EXPERIMENTAL DESIGN FOR EVALUATION
OF A CARPET CLEANER

Package Designs

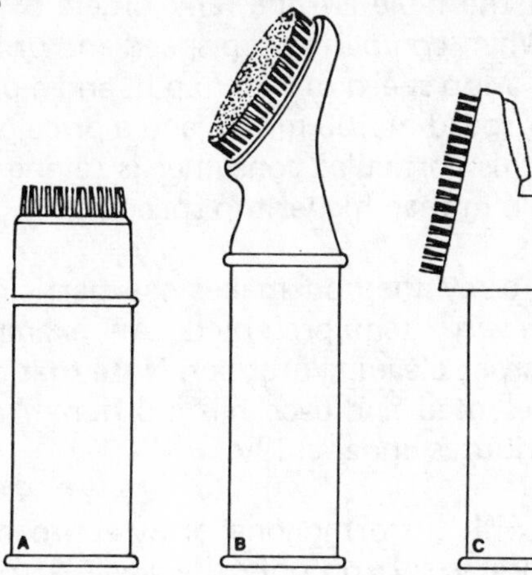

Orthogonal Array

Package Design	Brand Name	Price	Good Housekeeping Seal?	Money-back Guarantee?	Respondent's Evaluation (rank number)
1 A	K2R	$1.19	No	No	13
2 A	Glory	1.39	No	Yes	11
3 A	Bissell	1.59	Yes	No	17
4 B	K2R	1.39	Yes	Yes	2
5 B	Glory	1.59	No	No	14
6 B	Bissell	1.19	No	No	3
7 C	K2R	1.59	No	Yes	12
8 C	Glory	1.19	Yes	No	7
9 C	Bissell	1.39	No	No	9
10 A	K2R	1.59	Yes	No	18
11 A	Glory	1.19	No	Yes	8
12 A	Bissell	1.39	No	No	15
13 B	K2R	1.19	No	No	4
14 B	Glory	1.39	Yes	No	6
15 B	Bissell	1.59	No	Yes	5
16 C	K2R	1.39	No	No	10
17 C	Glory	1.59	No	No	16
18 C	Bissell	1.19	Yes	Yes	1*

*Highest Ranked

Source: Green and Wind [4].

pair-wise comparisons method, consumers need consider only two attributes at a time. This simplifies the task for test participants but requires that they consider a large number of trade-off combinations, often resulting in respondent fatigue. Again looking at Table 9.1, we see that entries in the table are the rank orders of preference for a single consumer. When comparing top speed and price this consumer gave a rank of 1 to a top speed of 130 m.p.h. and a price of $2,500, a rank of 2 to a top speed of 100 m.p.h. and a price of $2,500, and so on. (Incidentally, this particular consumer is saying that low price is more important to him than higher top speed.)

The orthogonal array method makes the participant consider *all* the attributes in *every* item presented. An example is shown in Figure 9.1 for a carpet cleaning product. Note that eighteen product "packages" are presented and each has a different array of the five components or attributes under study.

Our experience with the orthogonal array approach is that respondents tend to mentally sort on only the single attribute that seems most important to them and then casually order the cards without giving much consideration to the other attributes. A possible solution is to ask respondents to sort the alternatives into three or more piles (e.g., the best, OK, not very good) and then ask them to rank the product packages within each pile. This procedure results in respondents sorting small piles of items rather than a large number.

Calculating Utility Functions

Analysis of the data to determine each individual's utility functions is handled by various alternative computer programs that search for *a set of scale values for each attribute which, when added together to produce the total utility value for each combination, will correspond to the overall evaluation ranks as closely as possible.* Some of the simpler programs are modified forms of regression analysis that develop utility coefficients that best predict the rank order of the attribute combinations for each individual [7, 8].

Figure 9.2 presents an example of one person's utility function for the five attributes for carpet cleaners. To find this person's utility for *any combination* of attribute levels, one need only add together her utilities for *each* level of each attribute. For example, the product with package design A, brand name K2R, priced at $1.19, with no Good Housekeeping seal or money-back guarantee, has a utility *for*

Figure 9.2

RESULTS OF COMPUTER ANALYSIS OF
EXPERIMENTAL DATA ON
CARPET CLEANERS

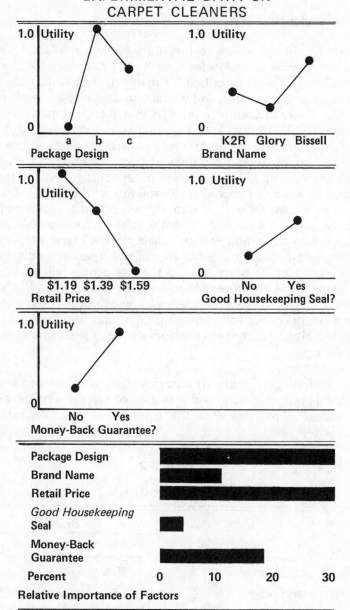

Source: Green and Wind [4].

this individual of 1.8 (.1 + .3 + 1.0 + .2 + .2). Similarly evaluating other combinations of levels will produce their respective utilities for the particular consumer.

Market Simulation Model

Using the utility values to prepare a market simulation model to "predict" choices is straightforward. In the example above, a variety of product packages (described by their attribute levels) can be analyzed by computing each individual's total utility for each product package. If we can assume that a person will choose the product with the greatest total utility value, we can predict each person's choice. If all products existing in the marketplace are evaluated in this simulation, we can obtain an estimate of brand share. While this brand share data may be learned through other sources, making this computation is a way of checking the validity of the simulation and of the utility values. Of greater import, new products (combinations of attribute levels that do *not* currently exist in the market) can be introduced into the simulation and their market shares projected. If a new product package has a higher utility for some people than any existing product, it is assumed that these people will switch to the new brand. It is thus possible to *estimate the new brand's share of market* and also to estimate *what existing brands will lose share.* This helps show how much the competition would be affected by a new entry and also how the new entry might cannibalize one's own existing offerings.

For example, in a trade-off study conducted by one of the authors on a food product, respondents were asked after sorting the attribute level cards, "What brand of this product do you now purchase?"

Table 9.2

DETERMINING MARKET SHARE

Method Used	Brands		
	A	B	C
Model prediction	46%	22%	32%
Reported brand usage	56	32	12
Store Audit	48	24	29

Independent data from store audits provided a "true" estimate of market share. Comparing the three measures of brand share—the model's prediction, the respondent's reported brand, and the store audits—showed *the model to be more accurate than reported choice* (see Table 9.2). This was not surprising since Brand C is a low-status brand. Apparently, respondents had a tendency to report using a high-status national brand rather than a low-status store brand (C). The ability of this model to predict market share so accurately supports the validity of trade-off analysis techniques.

Additional Simulation Uses

Playing the "what if" game with this same market simulation model provided some interesting insights. For example, a variety of alternative "new products" were explored:

1. Line extension of Brand A using its name but with a lower price

2. Line extension of A but with the same taste as Brand B

3. New product positioned as a store brand type (C) but having all other attributes of Brand A

Table 9.3 presents the predicted brand shares if each of the alternative new product packages was introduced. New Product 1 generates the greatest share but accomplishes this largely by cannibalizing Brand A. Although the combined share of New Product 1 and A is the greatest—73 percent versus the other new product possibilities—the profits would probably be lower since New Product 1 is simply a lower-priced version of A. New Product 2, offering a line extension of A with the taste of B, gained quite a share but again cannibalized A significantly. New Product 3, possibly the best alternative, produced a combined market share for itself and A of 65 percent indicated relatively little cannibalization of A, and drew much of its sales not unexpectedly from store Brand C.

In summary, the simulation aspect of trade-off analysis offers the chance to determine the effects on the existing market of new entries as well as the relative appeal of the various attributes. Whether or not these projections of market share with new entries introduced prove correct can, of course, be determined only through actual market introductions. *The assumption is that people will behave toward the actual products in the same way that they do toward the product descriptions (attribute level choices).* As we discussed earlier, reported choice and actual behavior often differ considerably.

Table 9.3
PREDICTED BRAND SHARES

| Market Situation | New Product | BRAND SHARE Brand | | |
		A	B	C
Existing market	—	46%	22%	32%
Market with New Product 1 introduced	57%	16	12	15
Market with New Product 2 introduced	36	27	15	22
Market with New Product 3 introduced	27	38	17	18

ADVANTAGES AND LIMITATIONS

While trade-off analysis is relatively new in its application to marketing problems, and is probably not as well understood as some of the other techniques, enough is known to cite some of the more important advantages of the technique:

1. In the frequent situation where consumers want the greatest possible amount of each of a large number of product characteristics or benefits, but where cost considerations loom large, trade-off analysis forces comparisons to show which features are *most* desirable when placed head-to-head with other features that are also desirable.

2. The relative desirability of each feature is expressed in quantitative terms.

3. It provides the most straightforward answer to the question: What *combinations of features or feature levels* are best for inclusion into the final product package—exactly what should the product be like? No other technique addresses this question so directly.

148

4. The technique enables an estimate of *market share* for any given combination of product features, plus the ability to trace the probable "draw" of the new product from each of several existing products

Conjoint analysis also has problems and limitations:

1. As noted earlier, there are problems in obtaining judgments from respondents. If the "orthogonal arrays" design is used, the respondent often feels overloaded with information and may simplify the task by basing the rank-order preference judgments on only one or two features. Conversely, if pair-wise comparisons are to be made, this results in a large number of separate rankings by respondents, leading to excessive fatigue. To help overcome these problems, a pretest of some sort might be conducted to identify features that are of little importance to consumers, so the final study can concentrate on the few features that are of key importance. Focus groups and simple correlation analysis are two possibilities.

2. Some features are easy to divide into categories (e.g., speed, price, warranty); others are confusing due to lack of objective standards (e.g., durability, styling, service). What do "good service," "smart styling," "very safe," and the like, mean?

Hupfer [5] lists several types of problems he feels are *inappropriate* for conjoint measurement techniques:

3. Products where relatively little conscious thought is given to the purchase: such products are usually purchased out of habit, with relatively little attention paid to trading off product attributes.

4. Low-cost products: the risk factor is low, and this again reduces the chances for weighing attributes.

5. When only one or two product attributes are known to be of primary concern to consumers.

6. When important product attributes cannot be manipulated; for example, manipulating price on certain products may face severe legal restrictions.

149

In spite of the limitations of trade-off analysis, it does offer the market planner a tool that for many product categories is the most realistic in its assumptions concerning consumer choice. Choice generally does entail making trade-offs of features, and people do have differing values or utilities that guide them in selecting between alternatives. Some recent, more advanced trade-off studies have used concrete stimuli rather than word descriptions. In one such study, product prototypes of business machines were presented to consumers. In another, prototype food formulations were served to respondents, thus giving them real information on which to judge and make their choices.

Trade-off analysis is not totally unlike product positioning in its general objectives. Both techniques try to identify the most important product attributes; both seek quantitative measures of relative importance; both search for characteristics of an "ideal" or "best" product. There are some problems for which either technique could be used. In general, conjoint measurement is preferred when attributes and categories/levels are specifiable in objective terms *and* when a real trade-off exists in the sense that *more* of one feature will inevitably result in *less* of another, due to price or other constraints. Positioning should be more useful where the most important features may not be known, or where they are stated in general terms in a positive way (e.g., durability, styling), or where no real trade-off may exist (as in the case of characteristics of many food products).

Trade-off analysis is in an infant stage. Advancements are sure to produce improvements that will make this one of the market planner's most useful tools.

REFERENCES TO CHAPTER 9

1. Green, Paul E. "Marketing Applications of MDS: Assessment and Outlook," *Journal of Marketing,* 39 (January 1975), 24-31.

2. Green, Paul E. "On the Design of Experiments Involving Multi-attribute Alternatives," *Journal of Consumer Research,* 1 (September 1974), 61.

3. Green, Paul E. and Vithala R. Rao. "Conjoint Measurement for Quantifying Judgmental Data," *Journal of Marketing Research,* 8 (August 1971), 355-63.

4. Green, Paul E. and Yoram Wind. "New Way to Measure Consumers' Judgments," *Harvard Business Review,* 53 (July-August 1975), 107-17.

5. Hupfer, Herbert. "Conjoint Measurement—A Valuable Research Tool When Used Selectively," *Marketing Today,* 14 (No. 2, 1976), 1-3.

6. Johnson, Richard M. "Trade-Off Analysis of Consumer Values," *Journal of Marketing Research,* 11 (May 1974), 121-7.

7. Kruskal, Joseph B. "Analysis of Factorial Experiments by Estimating Monotone Transformations of the Data," *Journal of the Royal Statistical Society,* Series B (March 1965), 251-65.

8. Luce, R. Duncan and John W. Tukey. "Simultaneous Conjoint Measurement: A New Type of Fundamental Measurement," *Journal of Mathematical Psychology,* 1 (February 1964), 1-27.

9. Tauber, Edward M. "H I T: Heuristic Ideation Technique," *Journal of Marketing,* 36 (January 1972), 58-61.

Chapter 10

EPILOGUE: THE BEHAVIORAL
MARKET STRUCTURE MODEL

The first chapter of this book presented a conceptual framework for the evolution of the process of searching for structure in consumer markets. The earliest model (Figure 1.1) was a simplistic one, showing how firms, products, and people were examined in relation to one another. Later models expanded on this by including consumer demographics and benefits *desired,* product characteristics and benefits *delivered,* and the influence of situation or occasion on benefits desired.

In this concluding chapter we will review the various technologies presented in this book as they relate to the more current conceptual model, shown here in Figure 10.1 (and introduced in Figure 1.2), which we have now named the "behavioral market structure model." We will suggest how each of the technologies examined in this book contributes to the understanding of each element or element linkage of the behavioral model. Finally, we will attempt to provide a realistic perspective for the use of market structure analysis in the market planning process.

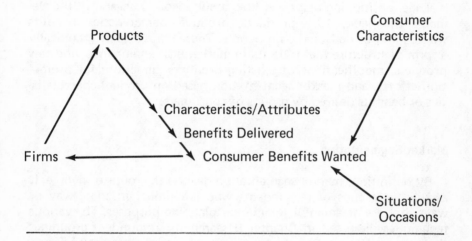

Figure 10.1

BEHAVIORAL MARKET STRUCTURE MODEL

Products

Consumer Characteristics

Characteristics/Attributes

Benefits Delivered

Firms ← Consumer Benefits Wanted

Situations/Occasions

Positioning Technologies

The various technologies used to position products/services/brands include multidimensional scaling (MDS, both metric and nonmetric), discriminant analysis, and factor analysis. Since these techniques were examined from a technical standpoint earlier, discussion here will consider only how they relate to the conceptual model.

While positioning techniques can do many things in many different ways, their usual objective is to position products in a space defined by either *product characteristics* or *benefits* or both. Thus, these maps show at a glance how much of each of the more important characteristics or benefits each product is perceived to *deliver* to consumers.

In addition, consumers can be located on a positioning map in terms of how much of each of the product characteristics or benefits each consumer *wants*. When respondents are spatially positioned in this manner, along with the various products rated, the result is a "joint product-person space." Examination of this space can reveal points (i.e., particular combinations of characteristics or benefits) where several respondents are located but no products, suggesting the opportunity to develop some new product to satisfy these hypothetical needs. Market segments can also be identified in product-person spaces by noting concentrations of respondents who all desire roughly the same combinations of product characteristics or benefits.

Thus, positioning maps can link simultaneously several of the elements of Figure 10.1—products, product characteristics, benefits wanted and/or delivered, and people. These maps display graphically a form of structure that is useful in marketing planning involving new products, modifications of existing products, directions for promotion efforts, and market segmentation based on product characteristics or benefits desired by groups of consumers.

Market Segmentation

By definition, market segmentation deals with groups of people; it establishes groups of respondents who are similar in some way or ways that are meaningful for market planning purposes. The various techniques discussed in Chapter 6 search for respondent groupings that are similar in terms of one or more of several elements of Figure 10.1—products used (and frequency of use), product characteristics or benefits *wanted,* demographic or psychographic characteristics, usage situations or occasions, individual perceptions or preferences for products, and any other descriptors that might be considered relevant for a particular planning need.

As pointed out in Chapter 6, however, while respondents can be segmented on the basis of any combination of these factors or even by all of them combined, it is strongly recommended that *only a single factor be used as the basis for most segmentation studies.* Using two or more factors simultaneously usually greatly obscures whatever segments might exist in either of the factors alone.

Just as segmentation can be performed in conjunction with positioning, as discussed above, so positioning can be performed in conjunction with segmentation. The recommended procedure is to first develop segments on the basis of whatever factor is considered most relevant for planning purposes; then, a separate positioning map is developed for respondents in each of the segments (to a maximum of perhaps two or three—any greater number of segments usually is not actionable for most types of products or services).

154

Figure 10.2
PREFERENCE FOR CANNED VEGETABLE SOUP

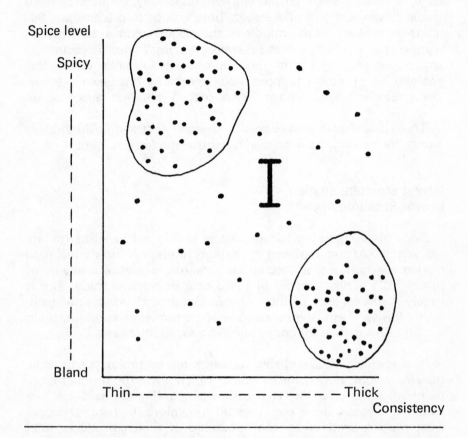

The present authors would even go so far as to say that, ideally, positioning should *never* be done without first attempting to segment a sample of respondents in some meaningful way (e.g., benefits desired). This could be based on ratings of the importance of various benefits to the respondent, on usage frequency or patterns, or simply on preference rankings for a group of products by each respondent. The reason for preliminary segmentation is illustrated in Figure 10.2 and discussed below.

Suppose the market for canned vegetable soups consisted of two principal segments: people who like their soup very thick and very bland, and people who like the reverse—thin with spicy flavorings. These two segments are shown as circles in Figure 10.2. If both segments are of approximately equal size, or even if both are reasonably large, building a single positioning map (especially a preference map) would have the effect of *averaging* both groups to produce an ideal point somewhere in the middle of the diagram, shown here as "I". *Note that a product with this composition would not be desired by any respondents at all,* in this hypothetical example. While most competitive product situations would probably not be so extreme, the researcher never knows when such a situation might occur.

Thus, it is almost always best to segment first and position afterwards, for maximum understanding of true market structure.

Market Structure Studies/ Benefit Structure Analysis

Since both market structure studies (MSS) and benefit structure analysis (BSA) are designed to explore consumer needs in broad market categories, both techniques emphasize several elements of Figure 10.1 almost equally in the course of a single study. This is largely a consequence of the scope and volume of information gathered. MSS surveys different samples of consumers at several stages in a study; BSA gathers all information in a single interview.

In particular, MSS probably focuses more on products and situations/occasions, noting the extent to which a specific product is appropriate for a given use or occasion (employing the item—use matrix). The typical study then goes on to explore the benefits people want from a product or from groupings of similar products. MSS clearly places greater emphasis on physical product characteristics than any other technique discussed in this book. Once the new product idea has been conceived in a general way, specific characteristics of its design are explored by the X-est and balanced madness techniques, using color wheels, shapes, object similarities, and the like. All of this work has the objective of endowing the final product with the physical characteristics that best convey the original intent of the new product idea (e.g., the happi*est* pickle).

In contrast, BSA places greater emphasis on identifying the specific benefits consumers *want for a particular use situation* (not from a given product or product type, although this information is also available). Then, by measuring the extent to which these benefits are or are not delivered in the same use situation, benefit *deficiencies* are identified. This same information is also developed for product characteristics, using verbal descriptors only. By studying the relationships of benefits wanted, benefit deficiencies, product characteristics wanted, and characteristic deficiencies, the market planner can develop ideas for new product opportunities that may be quite different from any product or service that is currently available.

Neither MSS nor BSA is particularly well suited for segmentation analysis, although both techniques offer data that could be useful for this purpose. BSA in particular is not very appropriate for identifying segments, since all questioning takes place around *a single recent usage situation* for a given respondent. Segments could, of course, be identified within a particular usage situation if the number of respondents was quite large (at least 75-100) for this situation. If the number of situations was large relative to the total number of respondents, as is often the case, the opportunity for meaningful segmentation based on benefits desired and/or deficiencies would not be great. However, some segmentation could be done based on patterns of recent usage of products in the given product type or category. Similarly, MSS respondents could be grouped on the basis of similarities of their item-use matrices.

Conjoint Measurement/Multiple Trade-Off Analysis

Trade-off analysis, though relatively new technically, has its origin in the early economic concept of individual utility functions. The economists' demand theory was based on the notion that each person had a utility for a given product (generally using a single variable—money). The potential demand for that product could be determined by aggregating each individual's utility function. This rudimentary notion is the heart of current conjoint studies.

Product characteristics/attributes, often including price as well as various physical or performance features (seating capacity, design shape, speed, etc.) are the variables most frequently used in these studies. Referring to Figure 10.1, trade-off analysis attempts to structure a market by revealing the relative importance of various attributes for a given product type. The products are represented by *combinations of attribute levels* (a car that seats 2, has a top speed of 120 mph, and costs $2,500.) Since individual utility functions are derived, the differences in attribute importance across individuals are measurable. Thus, for one person, speed is most important and price may be no object in car purchasing. For a second person, gas economy and purchase price are both critical, with speed and styling easily sacrificed. If enough people have similar utility functions in a product category, they may represent a segment for which a (new) product would have sufficient potential. Thus, clustering of individuals to form segments is possible.

Likewise, market share of brands or product types can be predicted using a simulation model which assumes that a consumer will choose the brand/type that offers the greatest total utility for him. Whether the conjoint measurement model (no interaction effects and a simple additive utility function) is too unrealistic to provide a valid market descriptive or predictive tool remains to be seen. Its strength lies in the basic notion that people are faced with choices and their purchase behavior reflects this in the marketplace. Further work is necessary to determine if people behave toward various combinations of attributes the way they do toward the "real" products and the "Gestalt" they convey.

CONCLUSION AND PERSPECTIVE

Regardless of the technique used, *the various objectives the market planner has for structuring markets should remain the focus of evaluating these and future efforts.*

A marketer needs to understand consumer purchase choices in order to predict this behavior and to influence it to his advantage. The appealing notion of the marketing concept—consumers with needs to which the marketer reacts—is too simplistic for planning purposes. Consumers' needs change over time as conditions change and in response to product offerings of firms [1]. Major product/service innovations (television, microwave ovens, bank credit cards, etc.) were not the result of a company's response to overt consumer desires. No doubt a latent demand for such items did exist but its existence is academic if this demand and the characteristics of the product to supply it were not directly measurable. For purposes of product positioning and repositioning, the present techniques are very useful.

To identify distinctly new products, however, these methods are less valuable because *they measure the world as it is today*. Whether the measure is consumer perceptions of attributes of various brands, preference for features or benefits, or even present product deficiencies (in benefit terms), these structures reflect a view of the market at one point in time—the present. Furthermore, peoples' knowledge of their "needs" past the early Maslow stages of food, clothing, and shelter (survival) is limited. A great many biases prevent the consumer from thoroughly understanding his desires [see 2]. Finally, the output from the variety of market structure studies outlined in this book provides only a starting point for product planning. As road maps, these studies enable the marketer to obtain an overview of the terrain, and provide some clues as to where people are in the mass complexity of their roles as consumers. However, the *actions* marketers must take and the related decisions—developing new products, advertising, repositioning, and so on—require a great inferential leap from the road map. The "ideal point" on a preference positioning map is a long way away from a concrete new product with all its trimmings on the retailer's shelf.

Therefore, in our attempt to position the market structure *process* in the context of product planning, we find that it primarily serves as a basic first step to help the innovator improve his odds of identifying new market opportunities. In short, while research can develop market structure, people develop products.

REFERENCES TO CHAPTER 10

1. Reynolds, William H. *Products and Markets,* Appleton-Century-Crofts Education Div. of Meredith Corp., New York, 1969.

2. Tauber, Edward M. "How Market Research Discourages Major Innovation," *Business Horizons,* Vol. XVII, June 1974, 22-6.